JAMES GALWAY

AN AUTOBIOGRAPHY

ST. MARTIN'S PRESS
NEW YORK

ACKNOWLEDGEMENTS

I would like to express my sincere thanks to the many people who assisted me to achieve the publication of this book. In particular, I would like to record my special thanks to Max Caulfield who carried the main burden of editing the material. My thanks also go to Michael Emmerson, who encouraged me to undertake the project and prodded me to complete it and to Audrey Lewis and Kathy Nicholson who dealt so valiantly with the many queries raised. My thanks are also due to Mrs. Muriel Dawn and my old friend William Dunwoody for the benefit of their recollections. And last but not least, to my wife Annie, whose patience and understanding during those long hours when I was engaged in the throes of authorship undoubtedly assisted me to complete my task.

The following sources supplied the illustrations used in this book. Illustrations not credited belong to the author: 6, John Francis; 7, G. Macdomnic; 8 and 9, Polydor; 10, Reinhard Friedrich; 11, London Artists; 12, Klaus Hennch; 14, RCA; 15, London Weekend TV Ltd

Lucerne, James Galway
1978

For information, write:
St. Martin's Press, Inc.,
175 Fifth Ave., New York, N.Y. 10010.
Manufactured in the United States of America

Library of Congress Cataloging in Publication Data

Galway, James.
An autobiography.

1. Galway, James. 2. Flute-players—Biography.
ML419.G28A3 1979 788'.51'0924 [B] 78-21403
ISBN 0-312-43965-2

CHAPTER ONE

For years I had been in some danger of exhausting Herbert von Karajan's patience. At one time I insisted on sporting a Frank Zappa beard and wearing trendy clothes, behaviour not at all in keeping with the then starchy traditions of the Berlin Philharmonic. Also my general attitude was considered a bit unorthodox; so unorthodox, in fact, that members of the orchestra nicknamed me 'the Berlin Phil's rocker'. I suppose I was a bit out of my head in those days and von Karajan's comment, 'Talking to Jimmy Galway is like talking to a man from Mars', more or less sums up his resigned attitude. Not that any of this had a direct bearing on the reason why, one day, he sent me a message at the end of rehearsal to say he thought that probably in all the circumstances it would be better if I did not accompany the orchestra to Salzburg for the Easter festival.

At the start of the season I had talked to him about the possibility of leaving the orchestra – such an idea is, of course, considered amounting almost to a breach of *amour propre*. The *Berliner Philharmonisches Orchester* is considered one great big happy family with Karajan a revered, towering father figure. Once you have passed through your probationary period and become a full member of the orchestra, you are really expected to stay for life. Nobody in their senses, it is thought, would ever want to leave the Berlin Phil.

Karajan's message, particularly as he had not deigned to deliver it in person, was hardly the most welcome news I have ever received. There is a special quality about the Maestro's Easter festival in his native city – you have probably heard the joke they tell there now: 'This is where von Karajan was born. Oh, and by the way, Mozart was born here too.' So I was disappointed to miss out. And also, I suppose, when it came to the crunch, I had mixed feelings about actually making the break.

Anyway, instead of trotting off to Salzburg with the orchestra as I had been doing every year for the previous six years, I rented a chalet with my wife Annie on the Angel Mountain, outside Lucerne. The Engelberg may seem an appropriate place to commune with yourself, but actually it is not as good as it sounds because it is a popular ski resort and there are usually too many people about. Annie, however, loves to ski and particularly *après ski*. Give her a long table in a jolly restaurant, people from Baden Baden or Hong Kong or somewhere like that and lots of noise and laughter and she always has a good time. Usually I just about manage to fit in, although I don't ski. So while Annie went skiing, I mooched about the chalet, gazed out at the scenery and from time to time did some intensive soul-searching.

Even at the best of times this is an awful thing to do to a Belfast Protestant who always has ideas about God knocking about in his head anyway. I scarcely needed reminding that the Berlin Philharmonic is the pinnacle in world music or that Karajan is the greatest conductor. To me the Berlin Phil was and is the greatest of all bands in every sense of the word, whether you consider the players either as musicians or human beings. I had always thought it a privilege to be principal flautist. But it really had become almost impossible to reconcile my aspirations with von Karajan's demands any longer. I was constantly disappearing at weekends to do solo gigs here there and everywhere, often flying over to London, for instance, then somehow scrambling my way back to

Berlin. Karajan had made it plain that in his opinion I 'no longer shared his mood', that I was 'off somewhere else'. And I could not deny it.

Since childhood I have been obsessed with the flute. I believe I am descended from a long line of wandering Irish musicians. Certainly, both my father and grandfather played the flute. People imagine that Galway is a typical Irish name but, in fact, it is pretty rare and I like to point out that there are only about a half-dozen Galways in the Irish telephone book – and one of those is a bishop. Anyhow, towards the end of the eighteenth century Belfast became a great centre of Irish folk music and it seems probable that one of my forebears drifted in from County Galway to play a harp, fiddle or flute at a festival and stayed on. Arguably, my great-great-grandfather, or somebody even further back, could have crossed over from the Mull of Galloway in Scotland, which you can actually *see* from Belfast Lough. Certainly old maps indicate that the city of Galway used to be spelt 'Galloway', so my name could be simply a corruption. On the other hand, I've never heard of many musicians, wandering or otherwise, coming off the Mull of Galloway, whereas it is next to impossible, I believe, to toss a brick in the air anywhere in County Galway without landing it on the head of some musician, even if it's only one whistling through his fingers.

Anyway, whatever my origins, I imagine most of my old neighbours back in Belfast still bless the day little Jimmy Galway took off for London and finally gave them a bit of peace. Living near our house must have been agony with me practising scales all day, or playing long passages of classical music which nobody could whistle. I have an idea that quite a few of them preferred the terrible crashings and bangings that drifted across from the birthplace of the *Titanic*, only a hundred yards or so away at Harland & Wolff's shipyard. Anyway, so far as I am concerned, playing the flute has been the greatest and happiest thing in my life and I daily thank God for the opportunities and talents He has given me.

Everybody, however, has a little bomb ticking away inside them, urging them to do this or that. And one day, inevitably, this bomb has to go off if you want to feel that you have realized your potential fully. Playing with the world's finest orchestra is a tremendous experience – one I would not have missed for anything – and one, I agree, that ought to be enough to satisfy the aspirations of most musicians. However, as the notes on the score lined up in front of me, and I lifted my flute to my mouth and heard the sound vibrate in the air, feeling for a brief moment in complete harmony with the world, I always knew that what I was enjoying was not going to last very long. In another second a veritable Niagara of sound was about to descend on me – the whole might of the Berlin Philharmonic at full blast, overwhelming my gentle flute. I got to the stage where I began thinking of the orchestra as one of those ancient Roman galleys. If you have ever seen the film *Ben Hur*, you will remember the part when the ship's commander tells the drummer to beat faster and all those guys have to start pulling the oars quicker. Well, that is how I had begun to feel.

What I really wanted to do instead was to stand up and let my flute be heard; to be listened to straight through from start to finish of a piece of music. Not to dodge the issue, I wanted people to hear *me*; I wanted to make my own music not somebody else's, not even Herbert von Karajan's. In short, I had outgrown most of the satisfactions available to me as a member of an orchestra. What I had always really wanted to do was be a soloist and the hankering now had become irresistible.

Karajan, of course, had known all about these aspirations of mine for a long time. During the six years I was with the Berlin Phil our relationship had been as father to son. At the start of the season, as I have said, I had already told him what I had in mind and that I would want to go. He had been full of kind and sound advice, telling me he thought every man had to do whatever he felt driven to do. He himself, throughout his life, had never hesitated to follow his own star. Yet, although he had indicated that he would not stand in my way, I also flattered myself that he valued my contribution to the orchestra highly and hoped that I would change my mind. Certainly more than one member of the band, with Karajan's blessing if not at his instigation, took me aside from time to time and tried to make me understand how lucky I was to be with Karajan and the Berlin Phil and what I might be tossing away in the shape of a career by leaving.

The umbilical snip had been inevitable, however, and now I sat in my chalet on the Engelberg trying to grapple with the problems that freedom would bring. For a start, I would no longer live securely within the warm womb of the Berlin Phil; even my material well-being might be in doubt. The sheer economics involved in the loss of a regular monthly cheque did not entirely escape my thinking.

Yet because of my background lack of money did not worry me unduly. The Galways never had had any after all, although now I also had to think of Annie and my young family. At the same time, I kept reminding myself, this was a moment for more profound thinking than merely worrying about where the next cheque was likely to come from; that would take care of itself. What was of greater importance was the whole question of my flute-playing and exactly what it was I had been doing with my life and what I should be doing with it in future. I even asked myself the question: what is the *meaning* of my flute-playing.

Slowly, then, novel thoughts (at least for me) began to fashion themselves in my mind. I looked back over my years as a professional musician and decided that my outlook had been far too competitive and materialistic. I had allowed myself to regard flute-playing more or less as a passport to the good life. I had been satisfied to trade technique for a standard of living, for plenty of steaks and bottles of wine, and had almost forgotten that there was more to music than that.

Sitting there thinking about myself and my purpose in life and finally about God – for, as I've said, if you're brought up in Belfast, then God takes up a lot of your thinking time – I decided I had been all wrong in believing that my role in life was simply to play the flute a bit better than the next fellow, to produce a better performance than the first flute in that orchestra or some other guy in some other orchestra. I decided I had allowed myself to get a bit screwed up. After all, I was never supposed to be in there fighting for some mythical Olympic gold medal for flute-playing –

although from the way I had been going on occasionally some people might have thought I was. What I had to do instead, I decided, was to make sure that I represented the composer properly to the world. Or to go a bit deeper, the composer's inspiration – which obviously came from God. It seemed to me I had been looking at the world the wrong way round, from the wrong end of the telescope.

I had put a lifetime of hard work and enthusiasm into making myself a good player. Yet I scarcely needed to be a genius to realize that something more than hard work or a run of good luck had lifted me from my very humble background and set me down in the world of great music and musicians; had brought me so much closer than I could have ever imagined to immortal spirits such as Mozart or Beethoven, by leading me to the very cities and concert halls where they had lived and worked. If it hadn't been for God, I kept reminding myself, I might easily have found myself stuck down in the Belfast shipyards, or some similar job, trying to handle something for which I had neither liking nor aptitude. When my mind began to career along this track, I found myself pondering the nature of good and evil and the tremendous force they both exerted in this world. I thought about how they often shaded together, so that when a man might think he was still on the right side he had, in fact, strayed from virtue. It seemed to me that Jimmy Galway hadn't been quite concentrating on such ideas and might have wandered a little. It was time to start thinking of prayer again.

As a boy, of course, I had been brought up with some pretty simple ideas about God and prayer. I thought about religion in very fundamentalist terms. Like most Belfast Protestants, I accepted every word of the Bible as *literally* true. I never stopped to think that the Book might not even have been written originally in English at all. I know all this sounds naive and simplistic but I never quite got the point that Christ Himself spoke Aramaic, a sort of lingua franca of a large part of the Middle East in His day, or that His words and ideas, first given written form in Greek and Latin long after His death, had to wait many centuries before being transcribed into the King James's version I was familiar with. Eventually, as part of my general education and widening knowledge, I came to know and understand the Bible better and also to recognize that there were many differing forms of prayer. It was while thinking along these lines that I came to the conclusion that my flute-playing had to mean something more than just a way of earning my living. I was like a man coming in from the dark, really, deciding there and then that in future I was no longer going to worry about whether I played the flute better than anyone else, but instead make sure that every time I played it, I played it as homage to the Creator.

Any atheist or agnostic reading all this may consider it a bit irrelevant. But what goes on in my head, I submit, is far from being irrelevant to my flute-playing. All I know now is that since that holiday on the Engelberg, my playing has taken on greater depth and quality. Before I sound a note these days, I dedicate the piece I am about to play, first to God and then to the composer. Jimmy Galway himself is kept out of it as much as possible. I try to remind myself that I am only an instrument, not unlike one of the glittering golden flutes I play on, fashioned for me by Mr Cooper of Clapham.

As a result, I usually surprise even myself. I am now convinced that my playing has taken on new colouring and depth and am quite sure that this is neither illusion nor a piece of psychological self-trickery. An artist invariably knows when he is fulfilling himself; knows how his performance ought to sound and how near or how far he has been from achieving what he considers perfection.

This change of thinking has affected far more than the way I play the flute. I am a much happier person, nowadays, more certain of what it is exactly I am supposed to be doing in this world. I have discovered a measure of serenity. For instance, I no longer kick senselessly against things, particularly if they do not go right for me. When a motor-cycle ran out of control in Lucerne and collided with me while I was simply walking innocently in the street, I did not give way to unreasoning anger, nor lie in hospital bemoaning my luck. I accepted what had happened to me with a philosophical resignation I think I would have been incapable of just a year or so earlier. I tried to see it all as part of an ordained pattern of events and even seized upon my time in hospital as an opportunity for further reflection upon where I was going.

Despite the pain and discomfort, I never at any time allowed myself to worry about what the accident might do to my flute-playing. It would have been easy to talk myself into deciding that my ability had been impaired or that my future as a soloist was at risk. While I lay in traction I knew that the enforced lack of practice would prove a nuisance, but I also knew that a bout or two of hard work would soon enable me to catch up. Meanwhile, I was prepared to put up with disabilities and discomforts and almost regarded them as a further spur towards spiritual awareness.

Indeed, on reflection I now view those days I spent on the Engelberg as, in a way, my own personal road to Damascus.

CHAPTER TWO

Carnalea is a pretty little inlet on the shores of Belfast Lough, a hop, skip and jump from Bangor, and the site of an important early Celtic monastery. Carnalea Street, on the other hand, as they say in Belfast, wouldn't fool a blind man.

Media men reporting from Belfast nowadays talk a lot about Protestant or Catholic 'ghettoes'. It is not a word I ever heard used while I lived there, but it appears to mean those square miles of little back-to-back parlour houses inhabited by people who work mainly with their hands and not their heads. That is, when they work at all. In my day, many of the people living in or around Carnalea Street, including my dad, didn't think of themselves as working-class but as the workless class. Anybody actually holding down a job was liable to find himself accused of being a capitalist.

I have asked Muriel Dawn, my first professional music teacher, what she remembers about our house. 'Well,' she said, 'it opened out directly on to the street. One cold tap, I suppose. No hot water. One little front room – a kitchen.

Two bedrooms. I remember when we used to go to talk to your parents about you going to London that your mother and father had to send you out into the street because there wasn't enough room for the six of us to sit down. But it really was a very respectable little area.'

The key word here is 'respectable'. Until the recent 'troubles', first-time visitors to Belfast invariably remarked on the great pride the inhabitants of these so-called ghettoes took in their little houses and how they kept them shining. Each morning the women of the area would scrub away at their doorsteps until it would have been safe to eat your dinner off them. In my view it is not possible to compare them with the great urban slums of England. For instance, until the 'troubles', Belfast had easily the lowest crime rate of any city in the United Kingdom and, in fact, lacked a traditional criminal class, unlike London. Most streets and houses reflected the overall respectability of their inhabitants, their basic longing to lead clean, decent, orderly lives. I am not denying that some men regularly 'got a skinful' on a Friday or Saturday night, but it is remarkable, even allowing for that, how little violence there was among the grown-ups in and around Carnalea Street. Warm and comradely, a more cheerful, lively place to live I cannot imagine.

Muriel Dawn was talking about No 17 Carnalea Street where I was brought up and learned to play the flute. I was actually born in another house in Carnalea Street but shortly after I made my début, on 8 December 1939, the Galway clan was forced to shift premises. What shifted them was the Luftwaffe which apparently singled out our house for a special air raid. It is possible that they were less interested in destroying our house than landing a bomb on the Belfast shipyards which you could almost reach out and touch from my back bedroom window. They may even have had the secondary intention of wrecking the railway terminus at the bottom of our street, which was a vital goods traffic link with Britain. But at the time it must have seemed to my dad as if they were after him personally. I often wonder what Hitler would have said to Goering if he had realized that the Reichsmarschall was attempting to wipe out a future principal flautist with his beloved Berlin Philharmonic.

It cannot have been anything much to laugh about at the time, however. My parents evacuated themselves to some relatives living about a quarter of a mile away – which was like jumping from the frying pan into the fire, for there the Germans planted a bomb right beside a large chimney stack belonging to a linen mill and brought it crashing down among the houses. I only heard about this afterwards, of course – I was a bit too young to realize what was going on. But it appears that I almost gave my farewell performance that night.

My father was a little guy – I'm not all that tall myself – with tremendous shoulders and arms; the kind of physique, in short, needed to be a riveter in Harland & Wolff's. Not that I can recall him doing an awful lot of riveting. I hasten to add that this hardly placed him in any special category; the decline in shipyard jobs in Belfast has been going on for a long time. I have an idea that my dad really only bestirred himself when the family badly needed something. He never complained much. Whatever his problems, and he must have had his share of them, he generally made the best of things and on the whole created a happy home for his wife and two sons. I certainly cannot remember any of us going short of anything important. There was always enough to eat; we had clothes on our back; there was always a fire blazing in the old-fashioned, black, iron range. If I wanted a gramophone, radio or flute, it always turned up eventually even if I had to wait a few years to get it.

I often meet people who want to sympathize with me because I come from what they like to call an 'underprivileged' home. It would be easy to be defensive about this and certainly for years, particularly after I first went to London, I suffered from a mild inferiority complex. But I also have to say that much of this talk of underprivilege seems nonsense to me. It never occurred to me, or anybody else living in Carnalea Street, that we were underprivileged. We were too busy getting what fun we could out of life to worry about that sort of thing. Perhaps I am an innocent. Did I not feel envy or resentment when I walked up the Malone Road (which is where the Belfast nobs live)? When anybody asks me a question like this, I feel they must have a slate loose. To me it would seem that they have little idea of what life is really about or what gives it substance and meaning. I am very much an apolitical person and perhaps if I had gone to university and met the kind of crowd who studied at Nanterre or the Sorbonne in 1968, I might be able to produce a right tale of woe. But the idea that a large house or a couple of extra bathrooms have anything more than a marginal effect on one's life, strikes me as minor lunacy. I am far from advocating poverty, bad housing, deprivation or anything else as a method of self-improvement and certainly over the past couple of decades I have gone out of my way, perhaps, to obtain my share of material things. But it seems to me that in the end material accessories add up to little more than the trivia of life. I suppose it is largely a case of what you never had you never miss. As for this inferiority complex; it is not until you find yourself invited to dine in houses that look like small palaces or to meet and talk to people who seem to know so much more than you do and who are part of this very nice background, that you begin to feel inadequate in some way. Nevertheless, I never at any stage felt envious of these people, although I admit I was impressed. I have tried to explain working-class feelings to people who regard me as a visitor from another planet. I tell them that everybody in Carnalea Street thought Winston Churchill was a marvellous fellow even though none of them had any real idea why he was so great. All they were aware of was that he smoked enormous cigars and rode around in big cars and lived in a big house. His head could have been a water melon for all they knew. But so far as they were concerned, a man who could afford big cigars and big cars had to be good. When I first met people from superior backgrounds, I suppose I more or less reacted naively. To some I must have seemed stroppy, vague, even unpredictable.

At any rate, none of us in Carnalea Street ever worried much about those who were better off, or ever felt any resentment. We accepted ourselves for what we were, which we thought was pretty great. None of us dreamed of moving into bigger or better houses. Even now, that is the kind of problem that comes right at the bottom of my list and I can honestly say that given the choice I would still wish to be born in Carnalea Street and be reared by the same mum and dad and to be, for better or worse, exactly the same James Galway that I am today.

Both my parents were musicians. My mother, Ethel Stewart Clarke, played the piano, although she never learned – or ever tried – to read music.

She worked as a winder in a spinning mill in West Belfast, but most people still remember her as a popular pianist. She played everything with a very curious harmony, but she produced sounds that most people considered very attractive. Certainly she was in great demand for meetings of the local women's guilds and that sort of thing and many of her old friends have told me that, once she stopped playing, attendances fell off markedly, that it was no longer the same scene at all.

Apart from the wonderful way she brought up both me and my brother George (who, incidentally, has earned himself a considerable reputation in Ireland as a jazz clarinettist and teacher), one of her bequests to me was a really large family. I have cousins all over Belfast, almost all of them from her side. They mainly run supermarkets and that sort of thing, but one of them once almost made it big as a pop star. Whenever I make one of my flying visits to Belfast, it warms me immensely to realize that I am part of such a large tribe. Kids I have never seen before come up to me on the street and demand to know, 'Are you Jimmy Galway?' When I admit it, they say, 'Well, I'm your fourth cousin.' I have yet to bump into any fifth cousins but no doubt there are a few hanging around.

My father, who was also called James, was more talented than my mother. He played the piano-accordion with several small dance-combos and enjoyed his fair whack of profitable engagements. His abiding love, though, was the flute. He was a member of the Apprentice Boys' Flute Band and was, in my judgement, a really good player. He understood harmony and knew a surprising amount of theory although he was never a 'taught' musician. Like everybody else in the Belfast flute-bands, he picked up the skill and techniques – and even learned the music itself – from fellow bandsmen. You learned from the fellow next to you, or the one a bit older than you, in the flute-bands. My father was lucky, too, in that he learned a lot from my grandfather, yet another James Galway, who came to live with us during the last years of his life. In his day my grandfather had been a famous flute-player – as had his father before him. I remember as a small child, when George and I were sent upstairs to bed, lying listening to my grandfather downstairs playing away softly on his flute. He had a few little special tunes of his own that he was particularly fond of and he would play them over and over again. Clearly he was a talented player because he taught many of the learners in the Apprentice Boys. Incidentally, the Apprentice Boys was one of the most famous of the flute-bands and won many competitions. It went out of existence suddenly one day when the Luftwaffe dropped a bomb on its band-hall – which is one you can chalk up to Goering.

I would have liked to have known my grandfather much better – my memories of him now are mainly of the many times he caught me stealing the sugar ration during the war. When he died, we had a wake, I remember. The essence of an Irish wake is that the dead fellow lies in his box in a corner while the neighbours troop in to express their condolences and then sit around the fire and consume a fair amount of alcohol. By the time everybody has had his share, the entire event becomes a great deal more endurable. You could even say that most people *enjoy* wakes, although in Belfast we never get up to the antics people get up to in the country parts of Ireland, where wakes used to be hilarious affairs. There are historically-vouched-for instances where a parish has *borrowed* a corpse from a neighbouring parish in order to have an excuse to hold a party. Not that my grandfather's wake was a solemn affair. Some of the amusement was apparently caused by me.

I was about as tall as a sixpence at the time – now I'm twice as big. It apparently upset me to see my poor grandfather lying there in the box (the lid of the coffin was still off, of course) and not being given anything to eat. Particularly when everybody else in the room was busy stuffing his face. So as a dutiful grandson I got a cheese sandwich and began feeding it to my grandfather. By the time my mother discovered what was going on the poor man had half a cheese sandwich stuck between his teeth. My father was heard to declare that as 'long as the chile [Belfast pronunciation] didn't waste half a bottle of whiskey, what does it matter?' This little episode and the fact that my grandfather wore a moustache and lived to a ripe old age and that he used to play the flute softly in the twilight is all that I remember of him now. I never knew my grandmother – she died giving birth to my father who was an only child.

I still have vague memories of searchlights over Belfast and the sound of guns – which is perhaps enough for anyone of my generation to remember about the Second World War. We moved away entirely from the York Street area of the city, and went over to south-west Belfast, to a house in Runnymede Parade which was much more modern. One thing I vividly recall is that we had electricity here. I cried my eyes out when my dad decided to return to Carnalea Street, this time to No 17, because it was nearer his work (I think he may have got a job in the docks at this time). I bawled because I missed that electricity. I hated the flickering, smelly gaslight after the bright clear light I had become used to.

Now, of course, I'm glad we made the move. I would not want to make pretentious claims for Runnymede Parade, but it was really more like one of those quiet and neat London suburbs; so quiet and neat that you sometimes never find out the name of your neighbour two doors away. Compared with the lively, vigorous, almost village-type of life that we led in Carnalea Street, Runnymede Parade had all the excitements of a busy graveyard.

To begin with, the immediate environs of Carnalea Street were full of characters. Not far away lived 'Buck Alec', a name that seems to have been passed down from generation to generation in Belfast. I don't know who the original Buck Alec was, but this one owned a lion. The lion didn't cause people half the anxiety Buck Alec did. He could not walk along the street when he had had a skinful without bashing somebody. I am told there was a Buck Alec who lived in Belfast back in the 'twenties who boasted it took half-a-dozen peelers to arrest him. The Buck Alec I knew was straight out of the same mould. We kids used to stand on a safe corner somewhere and watch him bash his way along the street.

Then, away up at the other end of York Street (which is one of the principal arteries out of the city), there was 'Corky'. She was an old doll with a cork leg and I don't suppose she was quite right in the head, but to us kids she was something wonderful. We hadn't enough sense to have sympathy for her condition or to understand her plight and I'm afraid we used to bait her unmercifully. We would yell 'Corky!' and various other expletives at her and then, when she turned in our direction, run for our lives.

Earlier I made the point that Carnalea Street and the other little streets around it were, on the whole, orderly and respectable. That was certainly true for most of the week – and particularly on Sundays, of course. Belfast used to more or less shut down on a Sunday. A lot of people like that sort of atmosphere; others take the view that morgues are for dead people. Perhaps it was because the place was so quiet on a Sunday that the roaring boys tried to make up for it on Friday and Saturday nights. That was when Carnalea Street and the area around got its share of the D. H. Lawrence's. This, of course, was only one side of it. You also had people like Sinclair Goudy who had a terrific voice and went off to work every morning bawling arias from *La Bohème* or *Pagliacci* – which is as good a way to be wakened in the morning as any I know of.

In later years even my own father used to come home roaring drunk every Friday evening. He was never violent or anything like that; just way off in that world only drunks inhabit. Although he was clearly spending money that would be far better spent some other way, my mother never protested. That was the way the world was then and particularly among us working-class. The wife never dared to argue with her husband; he was the boss. It sounds now like a good case for the women's libbers but my mother was essentially a happy woman and she and my old dad used to have many a good laugh together. We tried to make, and get, fun out of everything. Some people would be miserable in Buckingham Palace, others can live in Carnalea Street and still have a good time. Much depends upon your outlook.

There came a stage, however, when my father's drinking had started to be more than a joke. George and I decided it was all getting too much and that he was getting a bit out of hand, so we had a long serious talk with him (both George and I were into our teens by this time) and to be absolutely fair to my dad, it proved very effective; we had no more trouble. While it lasted though, our house, as I have said, could have come straight out of D. H. Lawrence.

There were one or two tough guys around, of course, apart from Buck Alec. The local 'skinman' (a Belfast term for a kind of freelance refuse collector who comes around looking for leftovers that can be fed to pigs) was one. In the next street there lived a docker who was also a holy terror. The docker and the skinman used to drink in the same pub and every Friday or Saturday night, after it closed, the two would repair to a bit of wasteground nearby and, in almost ritual fashion, belt the living daylights out of each other. They carried this on for years like a real religious ceremony. The only thing that ever stopped them was when Buck Alec happened to pass along; then he would give them both a right bashing.

I am sometimes asked if a small fellow like me with little or no pretensions to physical prowess and his mind full of what are regarded as artistic ideas, never had to put up with bullying. Or even, as can happen in tough areas, be regarded as a 'cissy'. It was never like that. To begin with, I was a bit of a mischief and could take care of myself pretty well. The important thing was to be a character of some sort. Even if you were only the kid who could throw a stone farther than the next, all the rest gave you a kind of respect. If you happened to be musical, then you were a fairly big fellow. Music was highly regarded in Carnalea Street and Cultra Street and all those other little streets; perhaps even more than the ownership of a lion, although that was regarded as a pretty big status symbol. All the grown-ups used to try and develop a character or personality of their own – Buck Alec's contribution was bashing people – and Sinclair Goudy got into the category through his singing. Every guy in the street, however, had his own act. One man, I remember, walked with a clipped, athletic, springing step. Another trundled along the street like a pint-sized John Wayne (whose ancestors, by the way, came from Belfast).

In a place like that, of course, there had to be a bully among the kids. We were lucky – we had about two or three. There was one fellow we nicknamed Tommy Tucker who used to give me a regular hiding. His father was away in the RAF and he rarely saw him and I think the combination of a hero father and one whom he rarely saw, gave him the idea that he should act out the role of a tough guy himself. I remember, too, that he had the most beautiful-looking sister who was both deaf and dumb. To this day, Tommy Tucker's sister constitutes one of those tragedies that will never leave my mind.

Anyhow, Tommy Tucker used to beat up everybody, almost as though he was hoping to make a profession of it. Whatever you said or whatever you did, there was no way you could avoid the inevitable. I remember one passage-at-arms I had with him. I happened to be combing my hair one day in a particular fashion – straight back – and he stood there watching me. Then he said, 'You shouldn't comb it like that, you know. You'll make it fall out if you do that.' I wanted to tell him that he was stupid, but I held my tongue. Very carefully I said, 'I don't think you're right there.'

'What do you mean? Of course I'm right,' he shouted belligerently. He sort of pursued the matter and before I knew it I had got one round the ear. He was a tough kid all right. When he grew up and went to work in a local mill, he was still violent. One day he picked a fight with somebody and just lifted him up and threw him right into a weaving machine. It was no joke; the victim had to have several stitches.

There was another kid called Johnny Reynolds, however, who lived just a few streets away and who was every bit as tough as Tommy Tucker, but was a very nice lad who never threw his weight around. Johnny took boxing lessons so a few of us decided it would be a good idea if we somehow managed to get Johnny squared off with Tommy. We finally got the two of them together in the street. Four of us took off our jackets and put them down on the ground to represent the corners of the 'ring'. And then the two of them started to lam into each other. Blood spurted freely from noses, but when the fray was finished Tommy had been taught his lesson.

There was yet another guy who used to stand at the corner and belt any of us who walked by. One day the idea occurred to me that what I needed was reinforcements. So I laid a trap for him and the next time he began cuffing me, I called out to my pals. Then all four of us piled into him and really laid it on him. As a final indignity we forced him down in the street and made him eat horse manure. The trouble with this guy, though, was that if he ever got you on your own again, he would have served you up for Sunday lunch.

There was a mild touch of the jungle about it all, although I took it in my stride. Much of our time was spent not only avoiding Tommy Tucker, but also Buck Alec's kids who were almost as tough as their father. There was also another group who relieved us of our money whenever we were packed off to a Salvation Army meeting.

We got tuppence, or fourpence occasionally, for the Salvation, but then had to run a gauntlet. To be fair to the kids who stopped us, they had their own curious code of ethics. If we had fourpence each, they took tuppence. If we had only tuppence, they left us with a penny. We were never given any choice in the matter, though – it was either hand over or get biffed. I was a religious enough wee fellow but I wasn't made of the stuff of early Christian martyrs. So the poor old Salvation had to go short.

During the war my father often left home to work in other parts of Northern Ireland. He worked in Londonderry, for instance, then the chief Western Approaches base. Whenever he went away, George and I became much more mischievous than normal. We became a couple of young hooligans. I remember I used to go around kicking other kids, for no reason other than sheer badness. I could also look a real scruff at times. Once I went round to the house of a lad called Tommy Moore, only to hear his mother yell out, 'You're not going to play with that Jimmy Galway! He never washes his face!' To avoid any reflection on my poor mother, I ought to say that she never stopped trying to make us keep our faces clean. But within seconds of a scrub, we would look like coalminers again.

I was one of the instigators, too, of what became known as 'the buttermilk gag'. A shop in North Queen Street had this big buttermilk churn and, once or twice a week, a gaggle of us would be sent by our mothers to collect pints of fresh buttermilk in jugs. Some of us got the idea of hanging around until other kids had filled their jugs, then holding them up like a mob of Dick Turpins and demanding to be given a drink. The idea of guzzling down gallons of buttermilk we hadn't paid for seemed the height of adventure. Eventually we refined this gag – we decided to drink our own buttermilk, then go home and tell our mothers that somebody else had bashed *us*.

We were constantly sharpening our wits. Once when my dad became mildly affluent, he invested in an old radio set so that we could hear music. He was a real scream with it. When anything went wrong with the set, he got down this old bicycle pump and solemnly began pumping the dust off the valves while the rest of us cracked up with laughter. He had it fixed in his head that dust was responsible for all the troubles with that old radio.

The set, of course, became the whole focal point of his life every Saturday afternoon when it was time to check the football results for his pools coupon. George and I would be busy kicking up hell about the place so he would say, 'Will yez away down to the railway station and see what time it is?', hoping to get us out of the way for a while.

It didn't take my brother and me long to realize how we could cash in on this situation. Every Saturday, therefore, shortly before football results time, No 17 Carnalea Street became holy bedlam. In no time at all my dad was saying, 'Here's a penny, then – will yez away down to the railway station and see what time it is?'

Clutching our pennies, we would run off happily, stopping to natter to about a dozen kids en route, climb over a few railings, annoy a few grown-ups, hop on and off a bus or two at the risk of being given one round the ear by conductors, before reporting back half an hour later to tell him exactly where the hands of the clock had been when we were at the station – which could have been fifteen minutes earlier. I suppose it taught me something about life. Don't ask me what, though; I don't know the answer to those sorts of questions.

CHAPTER THREE

As early as I can remember, there were always musical instruments lying about our house – flutes, piano-accordions, tin-whistles. If there wasn't somebody messing about with an instrument, somebody was singing. Whether it was because people didn't have the money to go to cinemas (there was no TV in those days) or couldn't afford radio or what, I don't know. But the whole street was like a musical pressure cooker.

For instance, the fellow who lived opposite us had won the Scottish Open Championships for bagpipes. Nellie Edgar had a banjo. There were two pianos in the street. There was also a miscellaneous collection of clarinets, flutes, accordions, trumpets and pipes and drums. Almost everybody belonged to a brass band or a pipe-and-flute outfit. Anybody who didn't own an instrument, sang instead. You could dander up the street, walk in the open door of a house and find people sitting around singing their heads off. It was a rich atmosphere in which to grow up and from the time I was a tiny nipper I was fascinated by musical instruments and felt compelled to find out how they sounded.

I heard plenty of good music – as well as the other sort – and I don't suppose many kids brought up in better homes enjoyed equal advantages. Not many, I suppose, learn to recognize the Mozart G Minor or the Jupiter Symphony before they are ten; I knew them both by the age of eight, just listening to my father play them. He was devoted to Mozart, as I am myself.

My father never made the mistake of trying to force me to *like* Mozart. If I had preferred to go into jazz as George did, he would not have objected. So long as you wanted to play music, that was all that mattered. Not that there was ever much chance of avoiding it really. I quickly graduated from 'Baa-baa Black Sheep', which I sang at my mother's knee, to Bing Crosby's 'White Christmas' and 'Rudolph the Red-nosed Reindeer' and then into the big cowboy tunes of the day such as 'Old Smokey' which we heard sung by our heroes, such as Gene Autrey or Roy Rogers, when we went to the Saturday morning matinées at the local cinemas. It was much later before we could afford a gramophone, but somebody once gave me a record of Al Jolson singing 'Mammy' which I treasured for years. One neighbour did have a gramophone and I used to run up the street to hear my record on this old wind-up affair. I would never have been satisfied merely to *listen* to music, of course. From toddler days I was fascinated by Dad's flute and, as I grew older, he found it impossible to leave it lying about the house. As soon as he turned his back, I would be playing it. He tried hiding it and then, when George and I kept finding it, he took it apart and hid the separate pieces. It made no difference; indeed, it only made the game a kind of musical hunt-the-thimble. It really maddened Dad that there was no place to hide it. Why he never simply belted the living daylights out of us, I can't imagine, except that from the beginning he set out to encourage our musical inclinations as much as possible.

He first bought me a mouth-organ, but if by any chance he had hoped through this ruse to get me to lay off the flute, he was mistaken. Nevertheless, I was as proud as punch of my new possession. The only trouble was that I could not play it properly. Everything sounded wrong. I soon discovered that it had only diatonic scales instead of chromatic. To play properly, you need semitones. With a mouth-organ which can only play in C, for instance, you cannot play anything in B flat. So I had to get one with a button on the side which, when pressed, allowed me to play half-tones. Dad paid £2 for it in the local music shop and I repaid the money over a period, although I now realize that he surreptitiously added an extra bob or two himself every week. So suddenly there I was, belting out 'White Christmas' and other favourites and having what I can only describe as a whale of a time. From the first, I discovered that playing music made me *happy*. When I am asked why I chose music as a profession, I can only answer that I had no choice in the matter. Music made me happy; it still makes me happy. As a kid I could sit down at two o'clock and still be bashing away at five, unaware of the passage of time. Mind you, I am not talking about scales and theory and so on; I hated that sort of things as much as any youngster.

Even while still fiddling about with the mouth-organ, I got into the penny-whistle – which, incidentally, I recommend as a first-class way for any kid to learn music. I was seven or eight when Mr Shearer, a neighbour, gave me a violin, and I owe him nothing but gratitude; it was a most generous gesture particularly as he had two clever sons of his own, but the trouble was that the old violin was rotten with woodworm. Dad took it along to a shop and got them to treat it, but the best way I can describe the resulting ensemble is to say that when I stood there trying to play, it was like something out of an old Charlie Chaplin film. Then one day the bow came apart in my hands – and that was that.

By this time, my dad, realizing that I had potential, had decided to turn me into a real musician and so he gave me some lessons in the rudiments of theory himself. But once I got the violin, he arranged that I should take lessons from 'Wee Dickie', a fellow-member of his band. Wee Dickie came round to the house on his motor-bike, had a cup of tea and then put me through my paces. It was all agony, of course. Scales bored me out of my mind and I couldn't stand the rigmarole and ceremony of getting the fiddle ready to play; tuning it up and so on. I preferred the tin-whistle; you just blew it and there you were, you had a nice time.

Brought up in my sort of surroundings, you develop a distaste for ceremony. It may have something to do with an informal way of living. Anyway, until quite recently I have disliked ceremonial occasions or anything of a formal nature. When I first went to college in London, I found it impossible to attend classes on time, for example. I didn't give a hoot and often turned up twenty minutes late. Later, when I took part in band rehearsals at the college, I would often decide to stay home instead and practise. My blood runs cold nowadays when I think of the way I used to keep all those fellows waiting.

I suppose other people regarded me as an extraordinary character. Not that any of my failings were due to a lack of parental authority. From the outset, Dad was heavy on the need to study theory and learn discipline. He drove me on relentlessly, always urging me to practise and to learn structures. I can still remember his voice urging, 'You get down there, boy, and make sure you get your letters!' Despite this, when I actually sat for my ARCM in London, I fouled everything up. The examiner that day was Professor Lloyd Webber whose son, Andrew, later wrote the music for *Jesus Christ Superstar* and *Evita.* I was just about to start my piece when suddenly all the lights in the Royal College of Music fused.

'Oh, it's gone a bit dark in here, hasn't it?' said Professor Lloyd Webber pleasantly and went over somewhere to see what he could do about fixing the lights. For some reason, perhaps because of nervous tension, I laughed. Although I had no intention of being rude, Professor Lloyd Webber decided I was laughing at him, so I began to treat the whole thing as a joke; talk about a mixture of an inferiority complex and sheer nervousness! Anyhow, within a few seconds, the whole thing had got completely out of hand and Professor Lloyd Webber was pointing a stern finger at me and declaring, 'Oh, go away then! If you don't want to do this exam, if you're not prepared to take it seriously, then you needn't!'

Other sensible young men, sitting for what is generally regarded as a critical examination, would have hurriedly backtracked, apologized and got on with it. I just bridled back and instead of trying to soothe the professor's ruffled feelings, turned on my heel and stalked straight out.

This was a critical decision for me and, as a result, I never really learned theory properly. Instinctively I rebelled at being forced to learn material I consider irrelevant to the way I play a flute. So I never passed any examinations. When people express amazement at this, I ask them to explain what having letters after your name has to do with an ability to play the flute. All that matters is what you *tell* people by playing.

Nor was it as though I experienced any difficulty with theory. In fact I was quite good at it, up to a point, but the truth was that I never wanted to do it. I had no interest in discussing the relevance of Bach's Fourteenth Sonata or how he came to develop it. It did not seem important to me. What did seem important was how to master fingering and difficult passages, and to learn to interpret a composer's music. Basically, I suppose, I was a traditional Irish folk musician and probably I would have remained so if I had not gone to college and crossed swords with some of the head men, which put me into a different category.

With all my experience, it is still possible that if I were asked to sit an examination in theory today, I would fail it. These theoretical parts come in various forms; you might be asked to harmonize something or write a little tune of your own, and it is on the cards that I could screw both up. There are other bits where they ask what certain words mean in French, Italian or German; the chances are that I would get by in this part, but only because I now speak these languages. Yet I still dismiss most theory-teaching. Possibly I am rationalizing things to suit myself. But I keep telling myself that all that anyone has to do to learn the theory of music is to read books. Whereas nobody can be taught to do what I do; you can either do it or not. I don't lack theoretical knowledge of course; I have picked up a great deal, probably more than could be learned in a college. Part of the trouble as I see it, is that many of the people who teach theory in the various colleges are not very inspiring. They may be as bored by theory as I was, but it is their job to appear enthusiastic and to arouse enthusiasm.

Wee Dickie did not lack enthusiasm, but I was at an age

when Gene Autry singing 'South of the Border' seemed to me the most beautiful sound I had ever heard. There were still a couple of years to go before I got a record of John Amadio playing the last movement of the Mozart D Major Flute Concerto and before I began to collect the records of Fritz Kreisler. Ahead of me, too, still lay that day when I first heard Isaac Stern play the Brahms Violin Concerto on the radio. Perhaps if I had heard Kreisler or Stern when Wee Dickie was trying to teach me the violin, things might have turned out differently. I might have been playing in a dance-band in Carrickfergus or Skibbereen or somewhere like that today instead!

A flop at the violin, then, I began on the flute. My first flute was nothing like the classical Boehm-system standard flute used by symphony orchestras. It was a simple six-key affair, a military-band type of instrument which was pretty standard around Carnalea Street anyway.

From the outset, the flute seemed easy and natural to me. I cannot remember exactly which tune I learned first but I suspect it was some sort of military march; they were great on marches in Carnalea Street. I do remember that I had to practise a few scales first but it wasn't long before I was enjoying myself. From the beginning, there was something about flute music that grabbed me. I could not stop. There was no other way in which I could so express myself. Obviously I was not cut out to be a mathematician, for instance, When I added one and one all I got was two; not some beautiful Einstein vision of the universe. Even when I played the same tune over and over again, it never palled. Each time I played a piece, I somehow managed to express it differently. Sometimes I felt myself reaching the heights; at other times, I seemed to plunge the depths.

Two particular memories remain with me from that time. When I was not playing the flute, I seemed to sit around a lot, just sort of staring vacantly at things, lost in thought. One day my mam was doing the ironing and I was sitting gazing into the fire. A neighbour came in, but I was so lost in my reverie that I didn't even notice her. Then I became aware of their conversation. The neighbour suddenly said something about the way I was sitting just staring and Mam replied,

'Oh, he's always *studying*'. It was her little joke, of course, but there I was, peering into the future, trying to imagine what I could be when I grew up.

A clue, possibly, came one day when there was a loud clatter at the knocker and my mother opened the door to be confronted by a gypsy woman offering her a sprig of heather. The gypsy talked on for a bit. Then, as I stood clutching at my mother's skirt, she asked if she could see my hand. I stuck out my mitt and she gazed at it intently. Then she said, 'You know, one day you're going to be a great musician.'

I don't imagine for one moment that she was capable of forseeing the future. Yet the words remained with me and in a sense may have helped to nurture the seeds of an ambition which I had already felt stirring.

CHAPTER FOUR

I suppose at times I must have seemed like a right little urchin; a bit of a ragamuffin. Yet when I compare my experience with the organized life led by many of my friends who came from better-off homes, I feel that it is they who missed out. Many of them seem to have been bunged away into boarding schools at an early age. I, on the contrary, lived like a free spirit with all sorts of things around me to spark off my childish imagination.

We never ran around in gangs, but rather in small cliques, brought together because we all lived next door or went to the same school. Once we were 'let out', as they say in Belfast, the world was our oyster.

'Let's go to Alec's bank and burn a few tyres!' somebody would suggest.

Talk about an adventure playground. When I see the kind of things they provide for children in Britain today, I am full of admiration for the caring thought behind them. Yet there is no way that these planned, carefully organized and relatively hygienic places can be compared with the Wild West landscape of Alec's bank. This was a gigantic rubbish dump whose bumps and hillocks could easily be translated by the mind's eye into anything from a backdrop for *High Noon* to a Nazi fortress being attacked by paratroopers. And the never-ending treasures! – the Aladdin's cave of stuff lying about! – old tyres, bicycle wheels, bits of vans and lorries, parts of ships' boilers, tin cases, old bedsteads. We would pick up an old tin, punch holes in it, start a fire, and sit around roasting potatoes. We would kick, batter, burn, break and vandalize to our hearts' content. We fought the First World War, and the Second World War too, on that rubbish dump.

When we got fed up with that, we trooped down to the bottom of our street and heaved half-bricks in the general direction of the stationmaster's office. Scattering once we had aroused the expected reaction, we then regrouped, climbed across a couple of roofs, went up and down a few steel ladders and along a gravel path and found ourselves in an old locomotive graveyard. In and out of ancient rusty locomotive boilers, driving wrecks at sixty miles an hour in our imaginations through the Rockies! It was paradise.

Not that it was all dirt and rust and rubbish. Less than half a mile away, was Fortwilliam Park where there were trees, grass and plenty of long sticks lying around out of which to fashion bows and arrows. When we had had enough of *that*, it was hop on a bus for a halfpenny and away down to Greencastle, the equivalent for us of Biarritz. Near the bus stop, somebody kept this huge black pig, covered in flies, and ritually we would halt to grunt and snort back at this poor animal and prod it if we had a stick. Then, under a small iron railway bridge we would stand and tremble in terror while a train thundered overhead and everything shook, particularly us. Next we would be out on the seaweed-strewn rocks, with the whole of Belfast Lough spread before us. There we would strip off and jump into the sea. How we avoided hepatitis or cholera or some even more awful disease, I have no idea. There were signs up everywhere advising people not to swim and even bigger signs warning them not to eat mussels, clams or other shellfish. We jumped, splashed, swam, involuntarily drank large dollops of the polluted water and, almost as though intent on suicide, ate every mussel, clam and shellfish we could find.

When I wasn't trying to poison myself, I seem to have been trying to break my neck. One of the glories of Belfast is the Cave Hill, a great half-mountain standing sentinel over the city, and part of the ring of hills and rounded mountains that surround it. On a clear day, you can stand on top of the Cave Hill and almost count the sheep grazing on the Mulls of Galloway and Kintyre across in Scotland. For us kids, the great attraction was the caves which can only be reached by doing a Hillary and Tenzing. One day, two or three of us managed to scale the perpendicular face and scramble into the second cave, only to find that we could not get down. In the end, the Fire Brigade had to be called out to rescue us.

We were ready for any devilment. What made my upbringing so different was that opportunities for devilment and mischief, in short, for adventure, were unlimited. In those days, for instance, nearly all goods traffic in Belfast was horse-drawn. So whenever a cart or van lumbered by, drawn by a jogging old nag, I and the rest of my bunch were out of our houses like arrows and clinging to the rear like a swarm of wasps while the driver yelled blue murder at us and slashed away with his whip. I've had many a stinging lash across the knuckles. But where can kids find that kind of excitement today.

There was no limit to the daftness. The father of one of my chums was a member of the B Specials, a volunteer body of reserve policemen, now disbanded. The B Specials carried revolvers and therefore my friend's father kept a gun and ammunition in his house. One day I decided we should fire this gun. Round to Tom's house, therefore, where we managed to unearth three bullets but, fortunately as it turned out, no gun. Undeterred, I suggested that we explode the bullets!

At one end of Carnalea Street in those days, somebody had painted a giant mural on a gable wall, showing British soldiers capturing a German soldier. Perhaps the best thing that can be said of this bit of art was that it was a heck of a sight better than most of the graffiti that usually covers Belfast walls. Anyhow, I suggested we stick two of the bullets between the bricks in the wall and then 'shoot' the third bullet at them. If all went well and the bullets exploded, Jerry would get his big toe shot off.

Well, we tried banging away with the bullet, then with a couple of bricks. After some minutes of this, Grannie Manderson came to her door, shouting and waving at us to clear off. This poor woman led a life of real misery, for every kid in the neighbourhood used her gable wall to play football or cricket – while some of the older fellows held a pitch-and-toss 'school' there. Anyhow, just as Grannie gave her first shout, I banged the bullet against the wall. This time, however, my hand twisted and the copper casing of my bullet struck the bricks. It exploded and I found myself gazing down at a shattered middle finger with my blood gushing out. When I realized I had shot myself, I let out such a scream that Grannie Manderson hurriedly backed into her doorway, certain the German Army had opened fire on her.

I was lucky I didn't lose my hand or even my middle finger. Clutching my wounds to my chest I ran for help and was brought round to the local Fire Station where the blood-soaked paw was washed and bandaged. There was no way of halting the bleeding, however, so the firemen rushed me to the City Hospital where I had three or four stitches put in my finger. By this time, somebody had managed to get my mum from her work and she collected me. I thought I had suffered enough by then but when my father arrived home in the evening the police turned up too. An incident involving 'gunshot wounds' had been reported to them. They more or less turned the house upside-down looking for hidden arms and ammunition and when my father explained what had happened, lectured him sternly about the inadvisability of allowing his eldest son to play around with live ammunition. If I ever did it again, he was told, I would be packed off to Borstal. The police were hardly away from the door when my dad had the strap down and little Jimmy Galway, mangled finger and all, was having the living daylights belted out of him. For weeks after that I could only play the flute by lifting off my middle finger and moving the other two fingers up, playing with my little finger instead of my third.

Years later when I was with the Berlin Phil and von Karajan was away, and we had a boring conductor instead, I once turned to the second flute and said, 'Hey, have you ever tried it like this?' To this day my trick fingering remains a kind of party-piece with me.

I was a pretty cocky kid, I think. Or to put it another way, I was irrepressible and irresponsible. I liked a laugh and a bit of mischief. I could be moody, of course, but I had a wide extrovert streak, too. Only recently I was back in Belfast for a funeral and got talking to an old neighbour. 'Hey,' I said, 'do you remember that kid, Robert, of yours? Wasn't he a terrible kid?'

'What!' he replied indignantly, 'our Robert a terrible kid! Listen, Jimmy – you were the worst kid in the street.' Then he reminded me how I used to tie the knockers of doors together, so that when somebody opened a door from the inside and closed it, it banged a knocker a few doors away and brought the people rushing angrily to the door. Or, as a variation of this, I would attach a bit of rope or string to adjoining doors, then give one of them a kick and run away to watch the residents vainly trying to get out!

I was absolutely fascinated, for instance, by this terrific doorknob on one of the houses opposite us, lived in by a stevedore called Bob Wilson. As I have said, everybody in the street prided himself on his individuality. (One man used to run a stall in the local flea market and went off every Saturday morning with a turban round his head, looking like a crystal-ball gazer.) Bob Wilson made his mark with this terrific doorknob. It intrigued me so much that once I knelt down behind my own door, stuck my airgun out through the letterbox and let fly. Ping! – I hit it about a half-dozen times and each time poor Bob would come to the door and look out, then go back in again, completely puzzled. I think I must have taken twenty years off his life that evening. In the end, peering through his window, he caught sight of the airgun. So my dad gave me one round the ear and that was that. Bob, in fact, never held a grudge. Every summer, when it was hot, he invited us kids into his backyard and cooled us down with his hosepipe.

I got on well with most people and held my corner. Some

of the kids used to yell 'Gawker!' at me because of my astigmatism (this is why my eyes dance around like leprechauns) and that led to me trying to belt the head off one or two people. But, at worst, that generally got you respect.

Looking back, I seemed to have the makings of a delinquent – although to be serious, I suppose there is a wide gulf between delinquency and the simple pranks I got involved in. Near our street were two establishments that intrigued us. One was Johnny Rankin's rag store which was full of old rabbit skins and things like that which we delighted in occasionally nicking, and the other was Mercer's Bakery where you could actually see them baking the bread as you walked past the window. Eventually I figured out that the back wall of Mercer's adjoined the top of our street. So a bunch of us got hammers and, when it got dark, knocked a few bricks out of the wall and got into the bakery where we proceeded to nick some of the cakes and buns. After this we would pinch a few potatoes, carrots and things like that from somewhere, light a wee fire and have a real banquet. It was days before Mercer's cottoned on to the fact that somebody was climbing in at the back and lifting their buns. The wall was then bricked up again and 'inquiries', as they say, were made, but we were never found out.

I wasn't half so bloody-minded or reckless, however, as some of the other kids. I remember when I was at secondary school, one of the bunch I ran around with there jumped aboard an electric bread van while the breadman was indoors somewhere having a cup of tea. Two or three of us crowded aboard with him and got it started. There was a long hill leading a half-mile or so down to York Road and we were travelling along nicely when our 'driver' yelled out in panic that he couldn't stop. It was like a scene out of a film. Behind us, as we careered crazily down that hill, raced the breadman, yelling blue murder. We were lucky we didn't get our ears thoroughly warmed that day, but somehow we managed to make our escape after running the van onto the pavement.

Most of the time, no doubt, it was pretty innocent stuff. There seemed so much to do. When we got tired of the engine graveyard and the rubbish tip, there were always the Belfast docks. We used to sneak in there and nick a few things like bits of wood or candles or something before the cops found us and threw us out. Near Alec's bank, too, was a piece of wasteground where one of the carting companies used to turn out their old nags to run wild before sending them off to the glueworks; this was real Wild West stuff, of course, and every now and then we would manage to corner one of these poor old stiffs and climb aboard and give it a canter, letting out whoops and hollers *à la* Gene Autrey or Roy Rogers.

Not far from the rubbish tip was the pumping station which took away the really dreadful effluent flowing down the Lagan from the city's sewerage. This, naturally, was where we went fishing, wouldn't you know. You should have seen those big, fat fish. They were almost as big as sharks. We used a bamboo stick with a needle stuck in the end to harpoon them. Then we took them home and told our mothers we wanted them for supper. With chips, of course. Most of the time all we got for our trouble was a box on the ears.

Yet I couldn't have been such a bad kid. At my first school, St Paul's, I was always one of the first to help the teacher. Part of 'helping teacher', of course, was getting to ring the handbell to call the class to lessons. Next to the flute, ringing that handbell was one of my greatest musical experiences. Later, when I moved up to classes three and four, I was always the first to volunteer to hand out pencils to the class on teacher's behalf. In case that sounds as if I were too goody-goody for words, I must relate the first day I ever attended Mountcollyer, my secondary school. The sensible way to get there was to walk along the street, then turn right along the side of a brickworks. 'Why should I walk the whole way round there?' I asked myself and decided to take the short cut. This involved shinning over a front wall, cutting through the yard of the brickworks, then climbing over the wall at the rear. As I climbed down the second wall, a helping hand assisted me. It turned out to be the hand of one of the masters who subsequently boxed my ears as a lesson in the proper way to get to school.

I wasn't quite as close to my mother in her later years as to my father. To me, she was just my mother and like all kids, perhaps, I took her for granted. She looked after me, made me breakfast, took me to school. She taught me the story of Jesus and I remember telling her that if I had been there, they would never have crucified Christ. I would have got hold of a pair of pliers and pulled out the nails. Even at that tender age, working-class Belfast kids were into things like nails and pliers.

I recall her as very good-looking. I once saw a picture of her when she was young and she was really terrific. As she got older, a lifetime of eating bread for breakfast, dinner and tea didn't do her much good and she put on a tremendous amount of weight which in the end led to a fatal heart attack. She was the family's sole earner for many years, of course. I remember the tremendous excitement in the house when a relative died and left her a battered old piano which, in my suspicious way, I imagine must have originally fallen off somebody's lorry. Although a music score remained pure Chinese to her, all anybody had to do was whistle or hum a piece and she could sit down and knock it out on the piano.

Old friends tell me that she 'was a lovely woman'; that she had this air about her that endeared her to people. It wasn't so much that she laughed and joked a lot – she had this twinkle in her eye. She was much softer than my father, which is why they got on so well; she knew his particular moods and reacted in her own way. She wasn't an intellectual in any sense and I would describe her personality as passive, but she mixed well with the neighbours and enjoyed a good laugh. She seemed to think I was a fount of good stories; one of her favourites was about the time I went down over the Border, into what was then the Free State, to get some eggs (they were rationed in the North then) and, in order to hide them from the Customs on the way back, hid them on the seat under my topcoat – which I then proceeded to sit on! This one used to really make her laugh.

As my father's frustrations over work increased and he took to drinking more and more, she handled him really well. It couldn't have been easy for her. I remember him coming home once and falling all over the kitchen. He broke everything in it, including one of those old-fashioned iron wringers. It was after this that George and I finally spoke to him. When he didn't immediately throw us out the window, we asked him to ease up a bit. But he had this strange Belfast mentality – no half-ways. He either drank or didn't drink. So he laid off entirely – and my opinion of him really soared because life must have been pretty hard for him at the time.

Neither my mam nor dad dressed very well, although my mother owned a very nice Sunday coat. Dad always seemed to be dressed in dungarees which he changed for a shirt and trousers when he came home where he proceeded to sit around and enjoy life in general. My mother was always capable of turning away his wrath with a joke. When he got out the old bicycle pump and began trying to blow away the dust from the radio valves, George and I always cracked up at him which made him stroppy. 'What are you two laughing at?' he would demand belligerently, but my mother would at once step in, make a joke, and in that way save us from a leathering.

They both seemed to have a good sense of fun. One night my dad decided to take a bath in front of the fire. For some reason, he forgot to pull down the window-blind properly and there he was, in all his manhood, splashing about and enjoying himself when two old biddies from up the street passed and caught sight of him. This sent them into hysterical giggles and they knocked on the window. Instead of becoming confused, he jumped out of the bath and, still starkers, made for the door as though to attack them. Immediately the two women rushed off up the street, still giggling and yelling. Dad was out on the street after them, threatening to chase them as they disappeared round the corner. My mother, who went out after him, almost burst her sides laughing. The two stood there in the street, Dad still starkers, laughing their heads off.

He died almost exactly a year after she did; I think he was broken-hearted. I wrote her date of death down in my Bible, the same one Dad used to use. It was one I got as a prize at Adam Street Sunday School where he packed us off so that he could read the *News of the World* in peace. When people die, relatives descend on the house like a pack of wolves – you know the sort of thing, 'Oh, I lent that thing to your ma', and so on. But two things I did manage to salvage – this Bible which lay beside my father's bed with the *News of the World*, and my mother's scissors which she took to her work every day. Those scissors more or less sum her up for me – someone who did the work, someone who earned the money.

My father, who was known either as 'Wee Jimmy' or 'Porky', was quite a character in his way – a real working-class hypochondriac. He complained constantly of headaches and was round to the doctor at least once a week for something or other. I don't think the doctor ever discovered anything really wrong with him, but he would give him a bottle of coloured water or a rub or something like that and pack him off home. Dad was always taking headache powders or pills which, in the end, did for his kidneys. It was like baiting a bear half the time in our house. Between lack of money, frustration and headaches, he had a rough enough old time and occasionally we got some of the backlash.

We became slightly antagonistic to each other later on because of his ideas on bringing up children and my lack of appreciation of what he was trying to do for me. He had a real leather belt and if he caught me up to mischief, there was always trouble. His way of showing you who was boss was to leather you one. He didn't bother to talk too much logic, but just laid it on right away. I remember once, when I was about eleven, going through his pockets to see if he had left any cigarette ends and coming across a cigar he had forgotten to smoke at some Orange Lodge 'do' the night before. It was the first time I had ever smoked a cigar – which I did while chewing an aniseed ball. At the time I told myself, 'This is the high point of your life, boy – sucking an aniseed ball and smoking a half-cigar!'; for a moment I felt like Cornelius Vanderbilt or Diamond Joe Brady. Then I got sick. When dad came home, he gave the air one sniff and demanded, 'Who's been smoking around here?'

'Nobody,' I answered, looking the colour of death.

He went immediately to his best-suit jacket, which hung on a nail beside the door, fumbled in the pockets and, not finding the cigar, came back with the belt and laid one on. 'Now, get upstairs and practise!' he ordered. But I was much too sick to do so.

One thing I must say about him, though; however stroppy it might have been between us during the day, it would always end up with me kissing him good-night and him kissing me back so that we could all go off to bed happy. He was really a very simple guy and always wanted to end the day well; he liked to think when he went to sleep at night that he didn't have an enemy in the world. When George and I were young kids, he came up every night and sang a little song to us before we fell asleep. He had this little rhyme about a flea – 'If they bite, squeeze them tight, they won't come back another night.'

I think he could have been a very good musician, if leaning more towards the entertainment side than the classical. After the Apprentice Boys' Band finished, he more or less dropped the flute in favour of the accordion which he played in dance-bands. He certainly taught himself to a fair degree of competence on both instruments. He learned harmony to such an extent that he could tell which chords were going on in a piece and could analyse a symphony. I remember him teaching me the Jupiter Symphony because he had to play it in some competition. He had pasted this piece of music onto a bit of brown paper so that it wouldn't get dirty or torn and he would play the theme from the symphony for me, at the same time humming away, 'bomp de bomp', trying to teach me. Afterwards he would sit in front of the fire and say, 'Mozart's the greatest composer, you know.'

He was a good leader. Put him among a crowd and out would come the accordion and soon there would be a sing-song under way. He and my ma would lead the singing, him on the old accordion, Ma on the piano, Dad bellowing away in a very forthright manner above the din. By his very enthusiasm he would encourage everybody present to join in.

There were, however, also some very sad things that I remember about him now. Once when he came back from Londonderry, he tried to get work as a dock labourer. In those days they had a green, yellow and red button system – green meant you were guaranteed work, yellow that you got some if there was plenty going, and red meant you stood no chance. He had got as far as his green button when one of the trade unions objected and the opportunity was lost. This got him dead peeved, naturally, and this was when he went through one of his bad patches. You saw his temper then; he was ready for a fight every five minutes. But there was this terrific other side to him – his tremendous love of music.

One of the things that made him supremely happy was that just before he died I took a Sunday off and went over to Belfast. At the hospital he was on so many drugs that he was really as high as a kite but he managed to recognize me. A couple of kids came in with a guitar and sang some hymns. Afterwards, I got out the flute and played. When the ward sister came along and I played the 'Carnival of Venice' and some other unaccompanied variations, he was fit to bust with pride. I had been making quite a few TV appearances just previous to this, so he died feeling that he had achieved something after all.

When I said good-bye to him, he thought he was going to be well again. They had only removed one of his kidneys, part of his liver and roughly a quarter of his bladder by then, but he was still convinced he would get better. When I said good-bye I knew I wouldn't see him again. Next day I was back in London. Then I was due to play in Dublin. After that, it was a big concert in Belfast with the Zagreb Soloists. He died the day before I got to Belfast. His doctor turned up at the concert and explained how he had had everything arranged to take my father to the concert in an ambulance. I don't suppose I ever played the *Four Seasons* quite the same way before or since.

He had this idea that a man should be strong, should be a tough street-fighting man. And he revelled in the fact that he was strong himself. During the later part of his life, he gave up smoking and gave up drinking and took to reading the Bible every day. I used to think, what a funny guy, reading the Bible all the time. Mind you, he also read cowboy stories and James Bond and that sort of thing. And since I found my new way of life, I now read the Bible every day myself.

Dad was obsessed with the flute when I was a kid. He thought playing the flute was the next best thing to believing in God. He would talk about it for hours on end. 'You should have heard your grandad do this,' he would say, as we listened to the radio. He was constantly saying things like, 'Did you hear the BBC Symphony Orchestra today – that flute was great?'

We went through this phase when I was trying to assert my independence and then his sense of humour would come through. Every time I came in at night, he would ask me where I had been. I wouldn't tell him. 'Who've you been playing with?' I wouldn't say. If he was in a mood, I'd just about give him the minimum answer.

One morning, when I had to go off somewhere, we were having our usual passage-at-arms after breakfast. 'Right, have you got everything?'

'Yes, I've got everything!'

'Have you got your music and everything?'

'Yes, I've got my music and everything!'

'Did you polish your shoes?'

'Yes, I polished my . . . . shoes!'

'Don't swear at me – do you know where to go all right?'

'Yes, of course I know where to go!'

He waited until I was half-way down the street that morning, me still hopping mad, then he leaned out the doorway and called after me, 'Hey, Mozart!' He had taken to calling me Mozart or 'big fellow'.

'What is it?' I yelled back.

'You've forgotten your flute!'

It absolutely doubled him up.

CHAPTER FIVE

My early struggles with the flute didn't amount to much; it all seemed to come pretty natural and easy. I suppose I got flute-playing mixed up with actually living – and then, of course, there was always my dad breathing down my neck demanding that I practise this and practise that.

Despite having no regular job, he used to amaze me sometimes by unexpectedly producing a wad of notes. One day he produced a whole £21 in notes (he kept the stuff hidden in a cupboard) and bought me a gold seal Selmer flute. 'That'll do you for a bit, won't it?' he inquired. 'Yeah, that'll do me for a bit,' I replied. In fact, it lasted me for about six months. At the end of that time I went round to talk to Purdie Flack, the local instrument repairer. Purdie took one look at my flute and declared, 'I don't think this is much good. But I've something here would suit you. Tell your dad it's only £30.'

Dad nearly fell off his chair. But when he heard me play it – I personally thought the gates of heaven had been opened – he realized that it was really something and might easily become a family heirloom one day. In fact, years later,

I gave it to the Galpin Society in Scotland to put on display with their historic collection of wind instruments.

What I wanted to do from the beginning was put everything I'd got into the flute. By perfecting my playing, I decided I could attain entry into heaven and I think this is what happened, because I actually do get there sometimes when I'm playing. Besides, the transition from penny-whistle didn't prove difficult. I had already learned to play all sorts of tunes and the fingering was similar. So once I tried out a note or two, simply trying to copy my dad, I was soon able to belt out easy tunes. Dad taught me from a little book called *The Simplicity Tutor* which contained a few easy melodies but mostly scales and studies. The fact that he insisted on my playing the scales and practising almost 100 per cent non-stop led to more than one row between us. I hated scales and studies – I wanted to play 'White Christmas' and 'South of the Border' instead. Like my mother, too, all I had to do was hear a tune once and I could more or less play it. So I began belting away at marches like 'Men of Harlech' or Orange tunes like 'The Sash' which I heard the local flute-bands playing. It is a kind of principle that exists with me to this day. If I know what a piece sounds like, I can play it better. Quite often while learning something, I listen to a gramophone recording to find out how it goes.

At first Dad let me get on with it quietly enough, although right from the beginning he was constantly on about practising; with him, the lesson was always on. Anytime he came into the house of an evening he would immediately pop at me, 'Right did you play your scales?'

'Yep.'

'Did you play your long notes and have you learned that other piece?'

If he ever caught me doing nothing for a second, it was, 'Do you want to do any practice, boy?' always delivered with a real hint of menace in his tone. I soon learned to beat it out of there before he got too stroppy. I'd run upstairs to the back bedroom I shared with George and there just play whatever I wanted to play. Even then he often wouldn't leave me alone. Once, I remember, when I had gone upstairs to practise 'Men of Harlech' in the scale of A major, I had some trouble with G sharp. Within seconds he was tearing in the door bawling out, 'There, you see. If you'd learned the scale of A major properly, you'd be able to play that!'

We couldn't go on like this, getting on each other's nerves. So he decided to send me to my Uncle Joe for lessons. Uncle Joe wasn't my real uncle any more than Grannie McAdorey was my real grannie. Grannie was the daughter of my grandfather's sister and Uncle Joe was her son. Grannie, who took snuff and had long grey hair which she did up in a bun like Queen Victoria and who would play patience or do jig-saw puzzles with me until the cows came home, was, I ought to say, a raving Ulster Unionist who would have shot any Catholic who came in sight. I thought Uncle Joe, who taught the Onward Flute Band, was a great guy; I think I really worshipped him. He worked in a pork butcher's and one of the things I always remember about him was the smell of salt. As a kid I was right into smells. Every time I entered a strange house, I'd pick up the smell: this one would be holy, this one dreadful, this one antiseptic and so on. Uncle Joe smelled of salt pork.

Joe owned a canary which was the joy of his life. He would come in after work, have his supper on the table, which Grannie used to scrub with bleach, and sit there talking to the canary. Then, after he and the bird had had a right old chat, he would turn to me and say, 'OK, young fellow, get your flute out.' I'd prop up my music card and the two of us would sit round the table and he'd sing the music to me. Then I would ask him to play the piece for me. He was quite nippy on the flute and really impressed me; very good with his tongue-ing and with a special way of attacking the notes which I thought very good. Most of the Belfast flute-bands had a very sluggish approach – but his attack was clean and crisp and I think I learned something there that I still retain to this day.

He showed me how to count – one, two, a one and a two – to get rhythm. He made me play scales, of course, but allowed me to play plenty of marches as well. One of the first things he taught me was called 'Children's Love' which I was very fond of and can still play today. I made plenty of progress until I ran into something in six-eight time. This was my first crisis and although I tried and tried, I couldn't master it. I remember one lesson ending with me flooding into tears. But spurred on by the thought of joining Uncle Joe's flute-band, I overcame the trouble. Joe was a very good teacher, consistent in how he taught. I remember him making me count some pieces right from beginning to end – just count them, so that I would get the rhythm right. He also dinned into me the importance of learning to *read* music – and not just becoming a player, as most of those in the flute-bands were, who simply played by ear. Although it was often hard, slogging work, I was so enthralled at the prospect of playing the flute well, of course, that nothing else mattered. Once I began playing, I was happy. It was like a form of meditation. Time flew.

The Onward Flute Band, which I joined when I was about nine, met in a room above a barber's shop just off Duncairn Gardens. I felt very special, going along there as the nephew of the bandmaster and conductor. By this time my imagination had been completely captured by these bands which marched like heroes about the local streets. I felt I would be a terrific fellow if I ever got to be a member of one of them.

Armed with one-and-sixpence from my ma (the subscription to the band was a tanner a week but they weren't always too particular about collecting the money and I think I still owe them about twenty quid), I attended every Tuesday and Friday nights for practice. Just before reaching the band hall, I had to pass a sweet shop where I always bought a chocolate bar. For me, life held nothing dearer in those days than a chocolate bar and playing marches with the Onward. We had sixteen flutes, bass drum, side drums, triangles and a cymbal and when all that little lot got going in a small room, you never heard such a racket in your life. 'Listen, I can't hear myself playing at all,' I complained to Joe. 'That's good,' he replied. 'That means you're in tune – everybody's in tune. You can only hear yourself if you're out of tune.' And he was right.

Shortly after I joined the band, we entered the melody flute section of the Flute Band League competitions which were held annually in the Ulster Hall, a big event in what you might call the Ulster folk-music calendar. The piece we had to play was 'Silent Valley' (about the lough in the Mournes which provides Belfast with its water) and I practised that piece until it was coming out of my ears. It turned out to be quite a thing to sit on the platform of the Ulster Hall for the first time while still only a kid, gazing down at a sea of faces. But I managed to keep my head and we won. The competitions went on all evening and the results weren't announced until about 2 am when the judge staggered out of the little box in which he had been locked up all evening with a bottle of Scotch to announce the results. I spent most of the evening in a local pub with my dad, drinking dozens of bottles of Coke and then clearing off somewhere else to eat fish and chips. I was over the moon, of course, when I heard the result and rushed home to tell my ma who, as usual, took it in her stride. She never flipped her lid about my successes; I'm not even sure she always understood their significance. Later, for instance, when I wrote to tell her that I was joining the Berlin Philharmonic, she replied saying, 'Oh dear, I do wish you'd come back to Belfast, get a nice job with the BBC orchestra here and settle down.' What a way to dismiss Herbie von Karajan and his band! My dad was a bit different, but even he wasn't all that good at handing out pats on the head. Belts on the backside, yes. But I could often see that secretly he was proud of me. Later, I know, he often bored the pants off his friends. It was natural, I suppose, and I'm glad that I helped to give him some happiness.

I found 'Old Comrades', 'Onward Christian Soldiers' and these sort of tunes dead easy to play, so in no time at all I was trying out variations. While the rest of the guys got on with the melody, I would break into rills and trills (which I was convinced sounded marvellous), much to their annoyance. Many of them still remain among my closest and best friends, but inevitably there was a tantrum or two. I had a terrible temper in those days, so one evening when they began taking the mickey, I clobbered one fellow with my flute -- and broke it! Floods of tears and recriminations all round, and then, when I got home, a touch of the Spanish Inquisition from my dad.

The Onward wore a dark blue uniform with red edgings and a red stripe down the trousers. If you looked closely at the cap and the rest of the get-up, you might rightly conclude that it was very similar to a Belfast Corporation bus conductor's. How they got into our hands is a mystery better left unfathomed. We carried little music bags over our shoulders and had a gadget for holding music clamped to our left arms. I found the whole thing glamorous and exciting. When we marched down Royal Avenue on our way to the Cenotaph for Remembrance Day ceremonies and envious friends called out 'Hey Jimmy!' as I passed, I felt like a film star.

The big event, of course, was 'the Twalth' – the 12th of July or Orange Day, when the Ulster Orange Orders celebrate Protestant William of Orange's victory over Catholic King James II in 1690. My dad always walked with his Lodge, the Imperial Temperance 929, and was always telling me what a great Lodge it was, as though it made any difference to me. I remember when I was very young being taken to the Field at Finaghy, on the south side of Belfast, and being so bored with the speeches and all these guys walking around with their banners that I howled the place down and had to be taken home. Even some ice-cream failed to appease me.

I really had no idea what the Twelfth was all about. To me it was just an opportunity to walk with the Onward, play the flute and collect what was really a massive sum for those days, £16. When you consider that the most my father ever earned in a week was £6 and that for the better part of his life he never earned more than £4, you will realize what an enormous sum this seemed at the time. For weeks ahead, of course, there would be a certain amount of preparation in the house. 'Get those buttons polished, boy!' my father admonished. On the eve of the Twelfth, it was 'Early to bed now, you've got a lot of walking to do tomorrow!' The idea of trying to sleep the night before the Twelfth was ludicrous. The noise and din in the working-class areas of Belfast were enough to wake the dead. Bonfires blazed to the small hours, often setting fire to infants, children, adults and houses, not to mention cats and dogs, so that you had fire brigades and ambulances racing through the city half the night. On top of that, special drummers kept up the steady rhythm of the great Lambeg drums – one drum is noisier than a fleet of Concordes and bitter Catholics have been heard to declare, 'You could hear those things from one end of the Dark Continent to the other.'

Then it was up bright and early – early, anyway – and off to the Lodge Master's house where the band would be refreshed with drinks; non-alcoholic in my case. All the Lodges and bands, with banners, sashes, drums, flutes, Lambegs, the lot, would rendezvous at Carlisle Circus and, led by the Grand Master, start off for the twelve miles' walk to the Field at Finaghy. There you ate white-bread sandwiches made the day before, drank orange juice if you were my age and something a bit stronger if you were older, and ignored all the boring speeches if you were able. People, most of them Catholics I think, came up and sold you ice-cream. When the level rose a bit – perhaps to four pints – some of the men grabbed the nearest wench and danced around the grass. This was the part I enjoyed most. I wasn't keen on the actual marching – not only because I got blisters. But some of the Lodges were very Protestant, with the philosophy, 'Don't enjoy yourself – otherwise you won't get into heaven'. Many of these people never really enjoy life until they die. Some Lodges, of course, were stricter than others. But when they marched on 'the Twalth', all behaved properly, walking along like good educated Protestants. I preferred the more hooley-like aspects of the day. For me this involved getting a blow on another instrument, such as a trombone, for instance. One year, I got to try out the bagpipes. It was like trying to blow an octopus.

In the end, I only marched to the Field three times. Then I got more sense.

It was very draughty inside our house, for none of the doors fitted properly. Sheets were changed regularly, but somehow or other blankets were only washed now and then. I never went hungry, but I lived principally on bread and butter. We only ate marge when the family was really hard up, and sometimes there was even jam. We ate lots of fish and chips – the big treat on a Friday night, pay night. I loved toast, but my father hated to see me eat it and used to warn me that it would 'thin my blood'! During the war we shook up the cream in the milk bottles to produce our own butter. We may occasionally have got help from friends or relatives, for I remember eating liver and sausages, roast beef for dinner on Sundays and, of course, an Ulster fry for breakfast – bacon, eggs, potato and soda bread (which I still yearn for).

Eventually I got a bike – two bikes, in fact, the second of which I took with me to London. At weekends, the special treat before going to bed was cocoa. For games, Dad taught George and me to play draughts and ludo. I always got peeved if Dad won more than three times on the trot.

The big thing was having to go to the WC at night during the winter. Ours was an outside job and it almost froze the bottom off you when you went out there with a candle. George kept two chickens there until my dad decided to eat one for Christmas.

When I was a kid the big love of my life was the local skinman's black-haired, black-eyed daughter. The skinman, whom I've mentioned earlier, had three terrific daughters, but the one with the black curly hair was the one that I particularly mooned over. Mr Blane carried on his work with the aid of a donkey and cart which together looked like something out of Walt Disney. His cart was continually filled with dripping rubbish, but nothing pleased us more than when he allowed us to climb up on the cart and drive the donkey. When we got home, we were always wet and stinking and Mother would half-kill us. For weeks I hung about outside the skinman's house, sighing for his lovely daughter.

In those days, I was the ultimate in fickleness, changing my girl friends every couple of weeks or so. A girl would be 'in' with me just as long as some image I had adopted from the screen lasted. Then when I saw another beautiful girl at the cinema, I would go for someone else. I began knocking around with girls at an early age, I remember – playing doctors and all this sort of thing in the little back entries of the houses on our street; just kissing and so on. I think I was three when I started going out with girls.

The image I liked to project, I suppose, was of laughing

little Jimmy Galway, the kid who got up to all sorts of derring-do, the one with the quick temper. But there is always another side to the mirror.

From my earliest years, I was constantly looking for a closer connection with God, seeking a way into heaven. The first book I ever read was called *The Life of Martin Luther.*

My search for a way to God began seriously when a guy called Richie Black, who lived in the same street, took me along to the Adam Street Gospel Hall Sunday School. When I got there, Richie talked me into reciting a little rhyme, which I've now forgotten, which made it sound as though I were a Catholic. When the teacher heard me spouting this, she nearly jumped out of her skin and demanded to know if I were a papist. 'No,' I said. 'Are you sure?' she insisted. 'I think I'm sure,' I stuttered in reply. At that age, in fact, I had no idea whether or not I was Catholic or Protestant.

When I was about twelve, I began trying out churches of different denominations in the city. My first school was St Paul's, near Carnalea Street, which was a Church of Ireland school, but for some reason I didn't like Church of Ireland services. They seemed dry to me and there was an atmosphere I was not happy with. Next I tried the Methodist Church at the corner of Henry Street, but that did not appeal either. Then I drifted along to the Presbyterians, but they didn't satisfy me any more than the Methodists. I never stayed with any church more than a couple of months until suddenly one day, down near the docks, I came across this beautiful church called Sinclair's Seamen. It is a well-known church in Belfast, although to this day I have no idea what denomination it is, except that it isn't Roman Catholic. I thought the people here very nice and their ideas simple and appealing and the name of the church also attracted me; I imagine I thought it was romantic. More important, possibly, was the fact that on the way I passed a terrific fish and chip shop where I used to stop and get four bags of chips on the way home from Sunday School.

The only church I dared not try, of course, was Catholic. Quite simply, my father would have killed me if he heard I had gone into a Catholic church; as for the neighbours, they would have gone out of their minds. Eventually, of course, the flute began to take over for me as a way of reaching God and from an early age I heard the voice of God in music. Flute-playing slowly brought me closer to what I wanted but was unable to put a name to. In my late teens, however, I delved into religion more deeply and at one point actually considered becoming a Catholic. Catholic churches appealed to me more than Protestant ones because they seemed happier places. They also had more decoration, their services were more ornamental and their altars were beautiful. The strange thing about all this religious attitude is that while I attended church regularly, my mum or dad never attended any church.

I remained religious when I first went to London and, indeed, was confirmed by the Bishop of London when I was nineteen. Then I slipped into an anti-religious phase, mainly because I began mixing with people who had no time for religion. I grew to like the things they liked, such as Impressionist paintings. I saw the same films, shared the same admiration for Fellini and Buñuel. For many years after, I was concerned only to lead a materialistic life, eating and drinking in the best restaurants, concentrating on increasing my possessions. It was not until I began to read the scriptures in a different way, towards the end of my stay in Berlin, when I began to understand and interpret their inherent symbolism, that I changed back. Then came that moment on the Engelberg when my thinking completely reverted. When I had what I consider a vision. Not a physical vision, perhaps, but a glowing concept of what life was really about.

To leap forward in time, I still think of myself as a Christian mainly because I was born one and would not want to change. If you grow up in a Christian community, you become part of a collective consciousness. Had I been born a Jew or a Zen Buddhist, I expect I would want to remain so. I now accept that there are many paths to God and a myriad different ways of communicating with Him. Music seems to me to be one of them. When Mozart was inspired to write *Idomeneo* or *The Magic Flute,* he was in touch with God. For me, one religion, one form of communication is neither better nor worse than another; the difference merely lies in that some people might find one form easier or more efficient than another. At the head of all religions is a Super Consciousness which people may reach through meditation, prayer or even just meeting together. For some, too much noise, too much talk, can create interference; often it is only when there is complete silence that the mind can reach out.

There have been two specific points in my life when I believe I came directly into touch with God. The first was when I visited a religiously inclined friend near Lausanne. He is now a farmer, but had studied history at the Sorbonne and had obtained an excellent degree. One day when teaching history at the University of Lausanne, he thought, 'These people don't really want to know history. And when it comes to it, I don't want to teach them.' So he went up a Swiss mountain instead, to live as a farmer and gardener. I didn't see him for several years. Then one day he took me up to his small farm and we sat around in this typical Swiss chalet, playing chess, smoking a few pipes and drinking wine. We began talking about the difference between good and evil and I told him I had difficulty distinguishing between them unless a person did something specifically wrong. He explained what he thought the differences were and read some Conrad to illustrate these for me. He drove the point home thoroughly, and that night when I went to bed I had two vivid dreams. In the first, I could see people behaving in a good or evil way; later when I reflected on this dream, I realized that everybody in it was a part of me.

After the first dream I woke up and told myself. 'This is ridiculous. Such a crazy dream.' Then I went back to sleep and this time dreamed about two very nice people. Suddenly I awoke again and thought, 'What a beautiful life it is,' and felt that if I could just put my hand on everybody who was in any way suffering or in need of help, then they would be much better people. It was an extraordinary feeling, as though a light were glowing inside me. It was very, very beautiful.

The second time was on the Engelberg when I came to realize how I, personally, related to the centre of the universe. I began to appreciate that to keep in touch with this centre, one had to be very careful, that it was easy to get out of touch with it. All this may sound faintly absurd but, as I said at the beginning, it has had a profound effect on my playing. Nothing pleases me more today than when somebody says to me, 'You know, Jimmy, you can hear God in your playing.' It delights me to think that in some small way I am a link between God and whoever is listening.

My father now felt I should be exposed to a more professional style of teaching and sent me up to a friend of his, a bookbinder by trade, called Ardwell Dunning, who lived in Roden Street. Ardwell was a wiry little chap, very smart in appearance and well into his seventies when he began teaching me. The lessons were held in Artie's kitchen with the music propped up against a milk bottle or jam jar. He was never gruff, but kind and patient, and I consider that he played an important part in my subsequent career. Uncle Joe had taught me how to read music and how to count. Ardwell Dunning was to take matters a stage further and introduce me to such complexities as harmony. To begin with he allowed me to borrow a beautiful flute, an eight-key Boehm-system instrument.

At each lesson I had to wade through pages and pages of *Steiner's Harmony*. What Ardwell taught me might have been rudimentary all right, but he taught the way only a great teacher would do, never hurrying or pushing me along. His handwriting was marvellous, and when he wrote down a chord it looked so very nice on the paper that I immediately began copying his script. He made me write out general harmony, saying, 'This is what I want you to do for next week – to write out all these chords.' He would then write some down – E flat minor first inversion, B flat major second inversion, chord of E flat in the root position. And I would write these down and bring them along for the next lesson.

I became so absorbed with my music studies that I got into trouble at school. I was then at Mountcollyer Secondary and one day the teacher caught me writing out this series of chords instead of a long list of rivers in China for the geography class. I had no intention of being bolshie or difficult but it seemed to me that there was no point to learning the names of rivers in China when I could be doing something useful.

One day Ardwell took me into his parlour and put on an old seventy-eight record of the Bournemouth Symphony playing the 'Oberon' overture. I was so captivated that I made him play it again – and then again. Another day I said to him, 'Look, Artie, why is it everybody else can play the flute louder than I can?' He gazed at me kindly. 'You know, Jimmy,' he replied, 'you're still just a small boy. All these other chaps you play with are grown-up, they're big and strong. I can only tell you that one day when you're big enough, you, too, will be able to play as loud as you want.' Which was very sensible and made me very happy at the time. His sister Winifred baked marvellous buns and, when the lesson was finished. Ardwell would give me tea and a couple of buns and then I rode back on the bus to Carnalea Street feeling on top of the world.

When I look back now, it seems to me that I was always fortunate with my teachers – whether they were teaching me music or teaching me in school. I was a dozy sort of kid at school, far from being stupid, but I went around in an apathetic and uninterested way. The first day I turned up at Mountcollyer, for instance, I couldn't even find the right way to my classroom. It was only after an hour or so that somebody discovered me in 1B when I should have been in 1A. Or vice versa.

James Stevenson, our English teacher, did a great deal to shake me out of my lethargy. We all thought he was a real scream and nicknamed him 'Stabo' because first thing on Monday mornings he came in and belted us all. He was a Glentoran supporter, while we kids supported the local team, Crusaders. One day the 'Crues' beat the 'Glens' and when he walked in we were in great form, banging desks and kicking up a triumphant row. Stevenson didn't say a word – he just went round the whole class of thirty-two kids and gave us all a belting. Another day, he asked, 'Look, do any of you kids believe in God?' When nobody admitted they did for fear of being thought a cissy, he said, 'OK, then, I'll read you a book instead of giving you religious instruction,' and proceeded to read us long extracts from *The Cruel Sea.*

Inevitably I got into arguments with the teachers because I was more interested in music than lessons. I was a really rebellious kid and once had a terrible row with Miss Gray, the French teacher. In the end she taught me a very nice Schubert song, 'Once a Boy a Rosebud Saw' and I discovered she had a very good singing voice.

The teacher to whom I owed most, however, was Malcolm McKeown who taught social studies. He was a well-known tenor in Belfast, a member of the Aeolian Singers, and every lunchtime accompanied me on the piano while I played some Bach sonatas. Mum saw me off to school every morning carrying my schoolbag and flute. I played the latter on the way to school, during the lunch break and on the way home again – and when I got home I sat and practised for hours. Mind you, it wasn't all Bach sonatas. The repertoire also included 'Oh, what a Beautiful Morning'!

As I became more immersed in music, I became less and less interested in ordinary schoolwork and my stroppiness and rebelliousness became even more pronounced, although on the whole I was fairly well-behaved. I never 'mitched' (played truant). My worst crime was unpunctuality.

Uncle Joe had taught me several light classical pieces such as the overture to *William Tell,* but within months my ambition had blossomed and I decided to join a bigger band, so I left the Onward and joined the Belfast Military Band (I later joined the 39th Old Boys with which I stayed until I went to London). The Belfast Military had everything – trumpets, cornets, even E-flat euphoniums and Wagner tubas, plus clarinets, bass clarinets and bassoons. I played the piccolo with them in a military-band competition held in the Wellington Hall. The test piece was the Coppelia Suite by Delibes which had a marvellous piccolo solo. When I first tackled this, I found it difficult and spent intensive weeks working it up. On the night, however, I surprised myself. I couldn't understand what all the trouble had been about; I simply steamed through all it and the guys in the band loved it, particularly when we won.

I was still only ten or so. Just ahead of me lay one of the most significant triumphs of my life; something I am still rather proud to remember.

CHAPTER SIX

I learned much from the Belfast Military Band. They had a particularly good flute-player called Hughie McMurtrie who had a wooden leg. Hughie really inspired me. I thought then – and still do – that he had exceptional technique. He once played the 'Carnival of Venice' for me and I thought I had never heard anything so lovely.

I was still just on the fringes of learning properly about classical music, of getting into it deeply. Light classics, arias, marches – and of course, 'Old Smokey'; these were the kind of pieces I was then ripping off on the flute. I had still a long way to go before tackling Mozart for instance; indeed I had yet to get switched-on to the classics. It was a transitional stage – in musical terms just leaving Jack and Jill and beginning to read Shakespearean sonnets.

It was not until I entered the Irish Flute Championships that those around me suddenly had an inkling of my potential talent. Nobody, of course, had ever thought of me as a prodigy; you simply don't grow prodigies in places like Carnalea Street. I was merely a kid who was pretty fly on the flute. My highest aspiration – and this also went for my parents, friends and relatives – was to play in a local street band. All my pretensions stopped there.

The championships were staged at St Anne's School, which lies within a half-brick's throw of Sandy Row, heartland of Belfast Protestantism and loyalism. There were classes for solos, quartets, sextets and just about everything else. In the solo section, there was a class for 10-13, another for 13-16 and an open class. With the boldness, effrontery, optimism – and sheer ignorance – that only a ten year old possesses, I decided to enter all three classes. I really had little idea what a competition actually meant. Under the tutelage of Uncle Joe and other friends, however, I worked up the three test pieces – 'La Favorita', arranged from a Donizetti opera, Rubinstein's 'Melody in F,' and a Viennese piece called 'Schön Rosmarin'. I practised all three as though my life depended on it. The Donizetti I decided to make sound as nice as possible – Uncle Joe showed me the rhythms. I had no idea how to play 'Schön Rosmarin' for at that time I had not been to Vienna and never realized that it merely means a special, charming, Austrian way of smiling at a girl. I simply got hold of a Kreisler record and copied that. Incidentally I find that the best way to learn music is to listen to the masters playing it. Throughout my career, I have used radio and records extensively. It is a widespread practice among professional musicians and no beginner should be ashamed to learn in this way. By this time, too, I had joined the band of the 39th Old Boys to which my friend Billy Dunwoody belonged, and Billy's father also helped me a great deal with 'Schön Rosmarin'. At the outset I was perhaps more terrified of the Rubinstein than the other two – but I listened to the Palm Court orchestra play it a few times on the radio and decided I had got the hang of things nicely.

So with hair brylcreemed, face washed, tie straight, a nice black double-breasted school blazer and the flute packed in its case, I travelled with my dad by bus to St Anne's, a large Victorian building with a statue of the old Queen in front. Up two flights we went, to an enormous classroom which had a platform. The competition was due to start at 7.30 pm and would last until the wee, small hours. There were ten entrants in each class. Each entrant was given a number, drawn out of a hat, to decide the order in which he or she played. There was no food on the premises but there was a good fish-and-chipper round the corner and at least fifteen pubs in the close vicinity, so nobody died for lack of nourishment. Half the time I didn't know what was going on, but every time my number was called I confidently strode forward, mounted the stage, stuck my bit of music (glued onto *pink* paper, for some reason) on the antique black music stand and proceeded to play my head off.

The atmosphere was both smokey and 'funny'. Half the time it was like fighting your way through pea-soup fog just to get to the stage. And the remarks: 'That's it, that's it!' – this was after I had played 'La Favorita' – followed by the dampener from somebody else, 'Oh, no, no good at all!' Everybody was busy airing his opinion with great authority and all the time I was getting more and more befuddled. I couldn't understand what they were talking about. One guy said to me, 'Yes, you play very good – but you've got a very bad tone.' *Bad tone*! It sounded as though he was telling me I had something wrong with my soul and wasn't going to get to heaven! I told him I thought the way I had played the instrument made it sound like a flute and what else did he want?

It was past midnight when the adjudicator finally clambered out of the white box affair where he had been closeted for most of the evening, to announce the results. Not a sound was heard, apart from the noise of even more furious exhalations and inhalations of smoke – by now it was like trying to breathe inside a factory chimney. For a while the adjudicator waffled on about 'some very good playing in this section' and then 'some very fine playing in that section' and fellows began biting their nails down to the quick. I merely wandered about like a kid who has paid his penny and got his chocolate, wondering why so many guys were smoking so many cigarettes and getting so edgy. The adjudicator finally got through the drums and duet section and reached the solos. He said something about 'one player here very good' and then waffled on again amid bursts of applause and loud coughing.

I cannot quite remember the order of things from then

on. He announced the lowest points in each section first, the way they do in the Miss World beauty contest. So we had this guy on 85 points, somebody else on 86, then 87½, then 95½ and finally he announced my number at 96¼. It wasn't until he announced: 'Boys' solo aged 10-13, third prize so-and-so, second so-and-so, first, James Galway,' that I realized I had won a prize. So I walked up onto the stage and was handed this little cup. A few minutes later he called out the winners in the junior section and this time I walked up and collected a bigger cup – again as winner. When he got to the open, all breaths were thoroughly bated. Yes, *James Galway*! Suddenly everybody was going out of their minds and pandemonium had broken loose. The look on the adjudicator's face was something to savour. When I collected the second cup, he looked as if he imagined he had been drinking too much. When I collected the third, there was a glaze to his eye as though he thought he might be hallucinating.

It was Shank's pony home then and 'Look, ma, look at these!' and up on the mantelpiece with the three cups. For days afterwards I bathed in a glow I imagine must be shared by Olympic gold medallists. When I look back on that moment now, however, I realize how wise and clever my parents were. They obviously knew I had done something special but just as obviously did not want me to lose my equilibrium. I imagine my old man dreamed a bit that I was Mozart come back from the grave. Anyhow it was then that he ceased to call after me, 'Hey, big fellow!' and substituted, 'Hey, Mozart!'.

Child though I was, I had already developed a certain desire to shine; or rather to do something really well in life. I feel sure that this was part of a desire to bring my Protestant upbringing to a proper conclusion without actually dying. That reads like a weird statement. But part of the Ulster Protestant ethic is to try to do everything to the best of your ability until you meet St Peter and he gives you the bad news. I believe that much of my desire to excel on the flute undoubtedly stemmed from this good, staunch, working-class, Belfast Protestant ethic.

It was partly through Billy Dunwoody that I first heard about the woman who, apart from my father, could be considered, perhaps, the person most responsible for whatever success I enjoy. If I had not met Muriel Dawn (and her husband, Douglas) I would probably have still been wrecking pianos in the shop where I went to work after leaving Mountcollyer School. Both she and her husband were professional musicians from Sheffield. Muriel was a remarkable person. Originally she had been a fine singer – she had sung in the Queen's Hall with Sir Henry Wood – but had later turned to orchestral work and, when she and her husband decided to come to Northern Ireland, she had joined the BBC orchestra in Belfast as third flautist. Wearying of the orchestral grind, however, she decided to take pupils. Billy told me that she taught the flute in a remarkable fashion which he understood was after the style of the French school of Marcel Moyse (who still remains one of my great heroes today). She and her husband lived in one of the posher suburbs of Belfast called Cherryvalley and one Sunday Dad made an appointment to call at her house.

Inevitably, of course, we got lost – turning up two hours late for the appointment. I was very impressed the moment I saw her. Her hair was snow-white and she was wearing this great Russian icon-like cross. The drawing-room was an eye-opener to me, full of beautiful paintings, most of them Irish. Like many English people who settle in Ireland for a while, they had become more Irish than the Irish themselves. Dad apologized for being late and in that very calm way of hers she said, 'Oh, never mind, let's have a cup of tea and talk things over.' She recalls that first meeting as follows:

> I never got to know your mother very well. But I heard about her playing, of course. People talked about her playing with great respect. It was your father we got to know well. I thought he was a grand person. Very worthy, a man of real principles. He turned up one Sunday morning at our house with you – two hours late. 'You've got to teach him, missus – and I'll pay you' and he poured some money out. He was terribly keen – the right sort of father to have. I think because you came from the sort of background you did, you got where you are. You weren't overlaid with a veneer and lacquer and ideas of the right

sort of this and that – you grew naturally.

I remember when Duggie and I talked it over after the visit and he inquired, 'What about teaching him?' and I replied, 'What's the point? – teach him to play in a flute-band? But where does he go afterwards? There's nothing he can do except play better than the other people in the flute-band.' But then you kept ringing up every day asking 'Are you going to teach me?' and finally Duggie went to see your headmaster at Mountcollyer. Duggie said, 'Look, this boy's just at a secondary modern – has he any brains?' And your headmaster answered, 'Oh, yes, he's clever enough – it's just that his parents can't afford the bus fares and other things involved in sending him to grammar school, even with a grant. And anyway he's got to get out and earn his living as soon as he can.'

Finally Muriel agreed to teach me. Sometime later, by the way, Duggie Dawn also agreed to teach my brother George who had never shown any interest in the street bands but was very talented. George was keener to play dance music and indeed has since taught himself not only to play the flute, but also the clarinet and saxophone. He's so talented, in fact, that he can play jazz and also the Brahms Clarinet Quintet and the Mozart Flute Concertos as well. One day my dad ran into Duggie in the centre of Belfast and asked him how George was doing as a pupil. 'Who's George?' asked Duggie, letting the cat right out of the bag. George had been going fishing instead of attending classes and Duggie had even forgotten his existence. There was an instant belting over that one.

For my part, anyway, I began trundling off to Cherryvalley every Saturday, clutching my seven-and-a-tanner (a lot of money in those days) in one fist and my flute in the other. I thought I had impressed Muriel when I first played a piece for her, but she staggered me by saying, 'Now, Jimmy, you've got to learn the basic method of blowing the flute.' I thought, 'fine', imagining that this would take about two minutes. 'We must now lay a groundwork that will last you for ever. So for the next month I don't want you to play the flute at all, merely blow the headpiece.'

For the next month therefore, I did nothing but blow that headpiece and make *embouchure* with lips stretched and the corners of the mouth down so that the top lip didn't come down in a sort of bite but I used the inside instead. While I kept wanting to play tunes, she made me stick to this dreadful routine for twenty minutes each day. Can you imagine it! By this time I was going out of my mind because I had thought I was a terrific kid, winning all these competitions and things and now I was being told, more or less, that I couldn't play the flute at all.

Then she told me to play just one note. On reflection, it was really something like Zen and the Art of Playing the Flute. The idea was just to blow the note until the note became me and I became the note.

Anyhow I had to produce this note and blow it normally and then to the utmost dynamic, the loudest dynamic, until I was ready to go up an octave. Then she said, 'But don't go up until you're ready' – in other words, don't go up the octave until the note is ready to break, then take it up an octave. She made me buy a book by Marcel Moyse, *La Sonorité* and do descending semitones and other exercises, including breathing. When I eventually left for England, she warned me, 'Now, whatever you do, don't let anybody change your *embouchure* and don't let anybody change your system.' I followed her advice so that today I have no trouble playing a low note loudly and a high note softly. I rather enjoy doing this because I know I do it quite well; better than 90 per cent of the other people in the world, anyway, which gives me quite a lift in its way. Under her tutelage, by the time I was twelve, I could play the B Minor Sonata like a veteran.

Muriel and Douglas Dawn created an enormous impact on the musical life of Belfast in the immediate post-war period. They had known many world-famous artists – Geoffrey Gilbert, Jack Brymer, Sir Adrian Boult, Sir Malcolm Sargent, Sir Thomas Beecham, and other lesser mortals. In 1951, Douglas was appointed Musical Adviser to the Belfast Education Committee and eventually became founder of the Belfast Youth Orchestra which produced such notables as Crawford Massey (Liverpool Philharmonic Orchestra),

Kenneth Montgomery (Glyndebourne) and David Strange Royal Philharmonic Orchestra). When he died I recall writing:

> I was introduced to the art of many great musicians through Duggie and Muriel. I remember very well the first rehearsals of the Youth Orchestra in the Belfast Technical School. The first rehearsals must have sounded very strange to anyone but amateurs – we had about 12 flutes, 8 clarinets, 2½ oboes, 1 cello, 1 viola and a few violins. I stayed in the orchestra until I won a scholarship to London – helped by Duggie. Duggie did something for the community in a very short time that others would require a couple of lifetimes to do. I shall never forget him as a music educator, clarinettist, pianist, conductor, composer and above all, as founder of the Youth Orchestra.'

It is perhaps a cliché, but these two people did open up a whole new world for me. Duggie would play me records of Jack Brymer or some other great artist and encouraged me to listen to the Promenade Concerts – I remember my dad and me sitting listening to our old radio. They introduced me to concerts of the British Music Society and other events and began widening my knowledge of poetry and painting. Muriel says:

> I remember that after six months you were away head of anything I could ever have done personally. I asked you, 'How much practice do you do?' and you replied, 'Whatever you give me.' I can't remember you ever having any trouble learning anything. You always seemed to just do everything and then go on and do more. Right at the beginning we took you to some British Music Society concerts and the way you appreciated the phrasing and shaping was astonishing; as was the way you appreciated the best from the not-quite-so-good. It was built into you – not something you acquired. You brought *feeling* with you right from the beginning – it never had to be put into you. You know, with some of the singers I teach you have to go inside and struggle to get them to release what's there. There was never that trouble with you.

The first orchestra I ever played with was the Belfast

Youth Orchestra which, when it began anyway, was a bit of a hoot. Miss Hazel Martin, who helped Duggie with auditions, always came along and tuned up the violins because all the kids were tone deaf. We met every Saturday morning in the 'Tech' and hacked our way through Handel's 'Largo' and similar pieces. Our first concert was held in the Floral Hall, Bellevue, a glorious setting on a plateau of the Cave Hill where we played Beethoven's Fifth and 'Where E'er You Walk' – the latter, I recall, had a marvellous solo flute part. I think Belfast has now one of the best youth orchestras in the United Kingdom. They played in Berlin while I was there and I played one of the Mozart Flute Concertos with them.

Duggie gave me quite a lot of useful instruction. My particular trouble at that time was that I used to play everything in my own way, whereas Douglas used to try to get me to play more within the rules. Within the rules of printed sheets of music, that is. There are two ways of playing music. You can play it exactly as it is written on the printed page, or you can let the youngster who is learning play a piece the way he *feels* it and then, if he goes too far wrong, correct him a little. The child then learns to play with something of his own personality and, if he is lucky, later on he plays with some of the personality of the composer too. Douglas used to tell me all these things. He would say, 'Now play this bit in time, Jimmy, you've got to watch this.' I remember once when he was making me play Bizet's 'L'Arlésienne' minuet, he broke in, 'No, look! This top note has to sound very nice and easy. We don't want it to sound too loud but nice and controlled and soft.' He made me play with a bit more nuance, more shade, more colour. He played a lot of music for me on his gramophone so that I could hear exactly how music *can* be played.

Any idea that my future might lie in the world of professional music had still not occurred to me. I only knew that a whole new horizon was opening up – but opening up to exactly what, I could not say. I think both Muriel and Douglas were undoubtedly aiming me towards a career in music. At school, however, I was heavily into bookbinding which had always fascinated me. I was skilled in drawing and graphics of any kind interested me. By the time I was fourteen I could sew, cut and bind books like an expert, producing works bound in leather and embossed in gold that looked quite stunning. When I was due to leave school, I applied for a job with a bookbinding firm, only to be turned down. I was dreadfully disappointed. This was the first time in my life that I had failed at anything I really wanted to succeed at. Sometimes, I believe, the more one tries to achieve success in a particular direction, the more one is certain to fail. In some odd way, you have to both try and not try before the gods look favourably on you.

It was vitally necessary that I secured some sort of job, however, so Duggie told me that there was an apprenticeship available with one of Belfast's largest piano firms. I applied, landed it, and for the princely sum of twenty-three shillings a week was given the task of learning to repair pianos as part of my apprenticeship as a tuner. Nowadays I like to describe myself as a former piano-wrecker because that is mostly what I was. I could somehow manage to take a whole piano apart and then put it together again – and still find myself clutching half the screws that ought to have been inside it somewhere.

Another job I had to do was clean the keys, carefully sanding down the ivories and then buffing them up until they looked as white as snow. There were also horrible jobs like cleaning out dirty gluepots.

I think Duggie Dawn's idea was that by working in a piano shop I was at least keeping in touch with the world of music. Cleaning out gluepots, however, didn't seem to me to have much to do with Beethoven or Mozart and I spent a lot of my time snoring away under pianos and in general keeping well clear of the foreman.

Fortunately the owner of the shop was as kind an employer as anybody could wish for, although we apprentices had to take a lot of stick from the piano-tuners. One day when a certain tuner was giving us a lot of the usual old guff, three of us suddenly jumped him. We had him on the floor with legs and arms flailing in all directions when suddenly there was this bull-like roar from the doorway. I remember looking up and seeing the boss standing there as though unable to believe his eyes. 'What on earth do you fellows think you're up to?' he demanded. 'This isn't a bear-garden, you know.' Like three sheep we rolled off our victim and shamefacedly slunk away into the shadows.

I spent a lot of my time in the shadows in that shop. I was leading an extraordinary kind of existence at the time really. My dad bought me a new flute for £30 and for a while afterwards money was so tight that not only did Dad stop boozing entirely, but I had to get a second job delivering newspapers in the evening for eight shillings and sixpence per week. I can't imagine how I found time to do this for I was practising the flute almost every second I wasn't in the piano shop. I was also busy with the Youth Orchestra and after work each evening would visit the house of a girl called Myrtle Ellis, where I would sit and listen to records or read scores or play the flute the whole night through. Myrtle was a marvellous pianist, her sister a very good violinist, while another sister also played the piano. I was then supposed to turn up at the piano shop at eight o'clock the next morning. Sometimes I made it, more often I didn't. But whatever time I got in, I was soon slinking away into the shadows and hiding under a piano somewhere, sleeping there until the boss or foreman or a tuner discovered me.

After I had been playing with the Youth Orchestra for a while, Duggie Dawn said to me one day, 'Jim, we'll have to get you into the Philharmonic' – he meant the Belfast Philharmonic, not the Berlin. In the end I played some Elgar with this orchestra but I didn't enjoy it and found the music so strange that I couldn't play it at all, so when a local BBC producer called Havelock Nelson, who had his own little semi-amateur group called the Studio Orchestra, invited me to join him, I quickly dropped out of the Phil. The group was very good considering they were part-timers and I really thought Havelock and his merry men were the absolute cat's whiskers. I played the *St Matthew Passion* with them and also made my first BBC broadcasts.

All this while I was still playing flute for the 39th Old Boys. At one stage I was playing with the Old Boys on Tuesdays and Fridays, the Youth Orchestra on Saturdays and Havelock Nelson on Wednesdays. In between I worked in the piano shop, delivered newspapers in the evenings, took lessons from Muriel Dawn and spent whatever time was left over either practising the flute at home or up at Myrtle Ellis's. It was just about as tough a schedule as I have ever faced.

In another sense, even that little list hardly gives a true picture of all my activities. To begin with, I was also madly in love with Myrtle Ellis at this time. She was quite a bit older than I was, but possessing this superior middle-class background and also studying at Stranmillis Teachers' Training College, she seemed to me to be the epitome of everything that was most desirable in a female. I was really smitten with calf-love on top of all my other problems.

The 39th Old Boys was a really exceptional band by the way and it is a rare occasion when I return to Belfast even now that I don't seize the opportunity to visit the old band room over on the Bloomfield Road where Etta Gault used to accompany me on the old wreck of a piano they had (and still have) there. Two of my greatest chums played with the 39th – Edmund Duke and Billy Dunwoody – and it is to these two men that I undoubtedly owe much of whatever success I enjoy. If it had not been for them, I would never have heard of Muriel Dawn and my life obviously would have been very different. They were also both behind the move which led to my father's approach to Mrs Dawn in the first place.

There was – and still is – a great deal of talent in the 39th Old Boys. Billy Drennan played a fine bass drum and his daughter Joyce was very good on the trumpet. His son Jim was an excellent pianist and I often visited their home where Jim would accompany me in a Beethoven sonata. Ray Stevenson was the brother of my old English teacher at Mountcollyer and played an F flute in the band, as I did myself. Edmund Duke was a really terrific flute-player and when I was about thirteen or fourteen, he was the great inspiration of my life. For a while Edmund, Billy and I formed a trio called the Zephyr Trio and staged a few concerts. I imagine we played some awful stuff. I do know that one day I took the terrible trio up to Duggie Dawn's to get his opinion and he cut us to ribbons. But he also cut our music repertoire so that audiences wouldn't actually fall asleep while we were performing. Inspired by this, we decided to give a concert in the Wellington Hall and I whipped up a whole crowd of our neighbours for the occasion. I can't imagine why any of them ever turned up, for they must have been thoroughly browned off by now listening to me playing the flute night and day.

Yet turn up most of them did. Duggie played the piano and I played the 'Chaminade Concertino', a showpiece for the flute. I had never known what it was to be nervous before but for some reason that night my face began to twitch uncontrollably and I thought I would never be able to get through my piece. When I had finished, every muscle in my body appeared to be shaking. At this time I was on a very religious kick and as obsessed with keeping to the straight and narrow as with playing the flute – which is saying something. Anyhow, at some stage of the proceedings I got it into my head that I was being punished for wrong-doing. However the only wrong-doing I could think of was smoking – which I had started at school. So still shaking with nerves and certain that the Lord had laid the fix on me because of my smoking, I took myself off to the lavatory where I proceeded to fish a cigarette out of my pocket and light up. Talk about being confused! To make matters even worse, after that I went at the weed even harder than ever.

One evening the Dawns suggested I accompany them to a British Music Society concert in the Whitla Hall, given by the Wigmore Ensemble. The flautist on this occasion was Geoffrey Gilbert who had once taught Muriel. I had never heard music played to such a standard before, and sat entranced. The Ensemble played the Debussy Trio and Beethoven's Serenade in D. At that time I was trying to play high notes softly and I remember how absolutely marvellously Geoffrey played it; he was total master of the flute.

What made that concert particularly memorable for me was the knowledge that this great man had actually asked to hear *me* play, and that if everything went well I was due to audition for him the following afternoon.

Something big was in the wind then, I sensed. But exactly what it was I didn't quite know.

CHAPTER SEVEN

The foreman in the piano shop was being his usual difficult self. For a moment or so it seemed as if he might refuse me permission to leave my post at some gluepot or other and walk the two hundred and fifty yards or so along Fountain Street, across Wellington Place and into the studios above another well-known music shop where I was to play for Geoffrey Gilbert. Finally, I was grudgingly given permission – 'All right, young fellow, but hurry up and get it over and get back here quickly.' Even that didn't end the pantomime. There was a row about what I was to wear! I was not to leave the shop in anything but my dirty old green overall-type of coat that was covered in the dirt and dust of countless scrubbings and sandpaperings of countless dirty old piano keys. It was like something out of Kafka.

I felt thoroughly ashamed of approaching a man of Gilbert's stature dressed worse than a tramp, but there was nothing for it. I found him and Muriel in a dusty studio or storeroom and I remember his opening words, courteously delivered, were 'Why are you late?' I didn't know what to say; I couldn't very well tell him that I worked for a man who would do anything to show his petty authority. Anyway, we eventually got down to brass tacks and I played him a Mozart concerto.

Muriel Dawn tells me that when I finished, Geoffrey asked her, 'How did you teach that lad to phrase like that?' Her reply was, 'I didn't – he's phrasing differently today because he heard you play last night. He always picks up the best out of everything he hears.' Geoffrey told her, 'I've never come across anything like it. I want to teach him.' Geoffrey Gilbert, of course, taught at the Guildhall School of Music in London. There was a long discussion about how this could be accomplished. My parents obviously couldn't afford my fare to London to audition for the Guildhall but Geoffrey briskly brushed that aside. I would not have to audition. On his word alone, the Guildhall would admit me. Muriel then said, 'I promise you I won't let anybody else have him. He will go to you.'

She could not have been more sincere in her words, but she was to live to regret them, because shortly afterwards she found herself in an impossible situation.

What was I like at fourteen? I cannot quite recall how I felt that day but after hearing what Geoffrey had to say, you can bet I was in high spirits. When I returned to the piano shop I have no doubt that, full of euphoria, I was ready to tell them all where they could get off and, in particular, tell the foreman what he could do with his sandpaper. Doubtless, too, I told them I was going to make the big time. In Belfast, of course, nobody ever believes anybody is going to make the big time, and when they do the scepticism reaches heights unheard of outside lunatic asylums – such as 'It's because his ould fella is a Mason', or 'It's because the Pope's trying to infiltrate secret agents into the Orange Order'.

Anyhow, I imagine I was a bit arrogant and cocky at times. Actually I had no self-confidence at all, and was probably busy covering up. Indeed, I never knew what real self-confidence was until I left the Berlin Philharmonic and decided to stand on my own two feet as a soloist. At fourteen I was neither apathetic nor indifferent to things, but I lived in a closed kind of world and was unaware of much that was going on. I was very shy, in fact, except when people entered my world – then I wasn't a bit shy, I can tell you. My world was the world of playing the flute and 'acting the cod', as they say in Ireland – that is, trying to turn oneself into a one-man entertainment in the interests of all-round conviviality.

I had a vague feeling that I was different from other kids. Other kids I knew didn't play the flute and go to symphony concerts and play in a band. Even a little later, when George started going to dances and meeting girls, I kept away from the dance-halls – not because I didn't want to meet girls but because I had developed this snobbish idea about music; I thought the popular dance tunes of the day were rubbish and that in some sort of way I might be contaminated by listening to them. I think I also thought that dance-halls were sinful.

Many things were troubling me. For instance, I could not understand why so many kids whom I didn't like seemed to be enjoying happy lives while I appeared to be miserable most of the time. I tried to do all the things I thought would help me to be happy. For example, I went to church and believed in God and hoped that by so doing I would find some sort of happiness or be led towards a better life. I realize now that I was looking for something from religion that religion is not meant to give.

I was quite unaware, of course, that certain steps were being taken on my behalf at this point that were destined to change the course of my life. Duggie Dawn had been endeavouring for some time, in fact, to persuade the Belfast Education Committee that grant support should be given to children other than those who were academically bright. He argued that there were talented children who, because of their home backgrounds, had either not been given a chance to take their O Levels or who had failed, and he pointed out that I lay in this category. It says a great deal for the intelligence and vision of the Committee that they took Duggie's point and a number of children, not necessarily academically gifted, but talented in other ways, were helped with grants. I recall playing the flute for a number of gentlemen in an old building in Academy Street, although I lived in such a curious world of my own at the time that I didn't realize *why* I was playing to them. The result, though, was that I was given a grant to enable me to attend the Guildhall.

Going there was much easier said than done. The farthest away from home I had ever been at this time was on a day-trip to Dublin. The idea of sending a fifteen year old off to London by himself obviously posed a problem. Duggie, of course, had some friends there, but Muriel for some reason was not impressed with them. 'Jimmy's definitely not going to go and stay with any of your friends,' she insisted.

The problem was both solved and further complicated when John Francis, who taught flute at the Royal College of Music, visited Belfast with a group called the London Harpsichord Ensemble. Among the engagements he fulfilled in the city was a lecture recital for the 39th Old Boys in the Albany Rooms where the sight of his gold-plated flute knocked me sideways. The way he played it also had the same effect.

Muriel invited John to her home to hear me play. I turned up for a lesson one day and was duly invited to play. As Muriel puts it:

> John Francis was thrilled to bits but I told him, 'He's going to Geoffrey Gilbert for lessons – and he's not going to anybody else.' That appeared to settle the matter, but next morning John Francis turned up at the house again and said, 'Look, I haven't been able to sleep all night thinking of that boy. I want to teach him.' I told him, 'No, you can't. It's all fixed up that he'll go to Geoffrey Gilbert.' So he said, 'When he comes to London who's going to look after him? Is he capable of looking after himself at his age – and never been away from home before?' Then he hesitated slightly and went on, 'If you let him come to me, I'll take him into my house and treat him as one of the family.' Then he added, 'I wish I were a great enough person to say I'll take him into my house and let him go to anybody else he wants for lessons – but I can't. If I take him in, I'll want to teach him.' Then he saw your father and your father came to see me.

My poor dad, of course, had really no idea what to do. He was a great guy in his way but he had no notion about making decisions – which is probably why he never got anywhere. I think I'm much the same but not quite so bad; every now and then I can actually reach a decision. Anyway we were all between the Devil and the deep blue sea. Muriel explained that Geoffrey Gilbert could get me into the Guildhall without an audition, but that if I went to stay with John Francis I would have to audition for the Royal College of Music – although I would unquestionably pass. Let Muriel take up the story again:

> Then your father came to see me and said, 'It's in your hands, missus, you decide.' That did it! Duggie then got at me – and I didn't know what to do but knowing what London was like and that you really weren't old enough to be on your own, I decided you'd better go to John Francis. So I wrote and told Geoffrey and got the most dreadful letter back. So I wrote him again explaining that the decision was entirely mine and that one day when you'd worked out your scholarship you could go to him. Geoffrey wouldn't have anything to do with me anymore until we met in Moscow in 1957 when he sat down at our dining table, looked at me for a moment and then said, 'I think we had better call it a day and forget about it, don't you?'

I was to live in John Francis's house in St John's Wood for the next three years, where both he and his wife, the well-known harpischord-player Millicent Silver, treated me as if I were their son. Duggie and Muriel visited us the next year and she recalls, 'You came in and looked part of the family and very proud of the fact. After the meal, one of the older girls came along and said, "Jimmy, I'll put your bath water on for you when you're ready" – and I thought, oh, what a difference from Belfast for him.'

The transition from Belfast to London was quite staggering so far as I was concerned. Although the centre of Belfast – Donegall Place, Donegall Square, the City Hall – had an incomparable air about it that even now I find quite magnificent, and some of the suburbs and surrounding countryside are glorious, London seemed out of this world. I used to ride around on my bicycle, discovering and marvelling at its grandeurs. Round the corner from us lived such notables as Judge Christmas Humphreys, Sir Arthur Bliss, Sir John Maude. The jump from a dingy little terraced working-class house bang next door to the shipyards, where people with handles to their names seemed to live on another planet, was enormous, but I like to think that I took it all pretty much in my stride, although by this time my inferiority complex had become as big as Buckingham Palace. It was under John's gentle guidance that I really began to discover the musical scene; I heard Leon Goossens play the oboe and Beecham's last concert, when the Royal Philharmonic was a truly great orchestra. John also took me to the Old Vic to see my first play – a Shakespearean production. John had quite a sense of humour. Although he owned a Rolls-Royce, he and I travelled over much of London on an old grey motor-bike, me freezing my bottom off on the back with no hat, and John up front with this furry type of hat the Muscovites wear. Even when we went to Covent Garden to see my first ballet – the *Prince of the Pagodas* by Benjamin Britten – we drove down on the old motor-bike. John was a real scream, a very genuine person and it amused him no end to park this battered old bike amid all the Rolls-Royces; I guess it's a special kind of feeling when you know you've got your own Rolls back home. I didn't understand the ballet at all but I enjoyed seeing the girls on the stage. John also took me to the National Gallery and the Tate where I was absolutely thunderstruck by William Blake. I spent many hours in the Tate on my own just staring at the Blakes and then I began to read his poetry. Certain that this man had been in touch with God if anybody had, I even mooched around to Broadwick Street to see where he had lived. Emotionally and intellectually I was broadening rapidly; even so I wouldn't claim that I was becoming a poised little gentleman. Still, I had begun to know the difference between a Blake and a Turner. I even read Milton's *Paradise Lost.*

John's house was a treasure-trove so far as I was concerned. His musical library astounded me. If you wanted to *play* Bach, he had his complete works; if you wanted to *know* anything about Bach, he had an encyclopedia which gave you whatever information you wanted.

It really is impossible for me to express the gratitude and

feelings I have towards both John and Millicent. If I wanted an extra lesson, John didn't charge me anything – I paid for it by washing the Rolls or helping Millicent with the shopping. One day, after I had half-broken my back washing down his Rolls, I asked him, 'John, why don't you sell that thing and get yourself a Mini?' Although they never actually paid for any of my clothes or footwear, they took only a nominal sum from my grant towards them. And when they went on holiday, little Jimmy was always brought along as part of the family.

As Muriel Dawn had predicted, passing my audition for the Royal College of Music had not presented any major difficulties. All the same, luck was with me, for I turned up that day without my glasses. 'Lord, I hope they don't ask me to do any sight reading.' I said to myself. Inevitably, of course, they did. I was asked to play a flute arrangement of one of the movements of the Bach G Major Cello Sonata. I didn't tell anybody I already knew this piece and just went ahead and belted it out.

To begin with at least, I attended the college assiduously enough (later on the whole thing became a scream – you'd ask a friend to mark you present and once this idea caught on everybody was at it so that in the end only about four people were turning up for the lessons. Not that I was slacking; I was busy at John Francis's place getting on with what I considered the main job, learning to *play* the flute, not listening to a lot of theory or to the history of music, or other codswallop). During my first term I was put into the college's second orchestra; during my second, I made the first. I wouldn't say the standard was all that marvellous, but it seemed pretty impressive to me in those days.

One of the first things that happened to me was that I fell in love with a girl in the orchestra called Brigid Rainger. I was still so shy, however, that I never told her and, possibly, if she reads this book, she will get quite a shock. At that, I'm not quite sure whether I fell in love with her or with her violin or with a mixture of the two. She played the Beethoven Violin Concerto and from the first time I heard it I couldn't stop singing it. Still today, whenever I hear it played I think of Brigid.

Even when I was still in college, too, I had the idea that I did not want to be a member of an orchestra but might become a soloist. However, everybody said, 'What, the flute! Forget it! Get yourself a job in an orchestra. There's nothing to play on the flute, you'll never make it.' To demonstrate how daft I was, other students were asked to play the Beethoven Violin Concerto or the Rachmaninov Piano Concerto. 'Mozart's flute concertos are not to be compared with these,' I was told. So I more or less gave up all hope of being a soloist, but I still went ahead and learned the solo repertoire all the same. John Francis, of course, was terrific at this time. He made me get my nose down into all these orchestral books and learn the flute extracts, and the grounding I got from him then stood me in good stead later. For instance, when I auditioned for the London Symphony, the first piece they asked me to play was one I had learned from him. I simply raced through it like a virtuoso.

On the whole I found college useful and worthwhile, though for the life of me I still cannot understand why anybody in their right mind would want to listen to lectures on the history of music. My view is that most of the men who give these lectures are disappointed composers and instrumentalists and I think they ought to do something else with their time. There were marvellous exceptions, of course. One was Harry Stubbs who not only taught me harmony but how to recognize the time signature of a piece because of the *feel.* He really inspired me, showing me the hidden language of music. With too many it's a question of churning out musicians as though they were shorthand-typists who can write shorthand at 130 words a minute and type at 70 but lack any feeling for, or knowledge of, what they are writing. Ernest Hall, who took the wind section, was also an important influence. He had played with most of the famous orchestras in England and knew how each piece should sound. When I wanted to know how something should go, he would pick up his trumpet and show me.

While Muriel Dawn was still teaching me, she had given me some studies arranged for the flute by the great flautist Marcel Moyse, transposed from piano studies by Cramer. One day John Francis handed me a record by Marcel Moyse which just stopped me in my tracks. I had simply never heard anybody play the flute like that before. 'So what's special about this guy?' I asked John. He couldn't quite explain it and I couldn't figure it out, so, reverting to my old habits, I did the next best thing and simply copied him. That was fine except that I thenceforward played everything like Marcel Moyse. I remember one day going in for a lesson with John and playing a Bach sonata. At the end, John complained, 'You know, Jimmy, that sounds like Moyse.'

'Yes,' I agreed, 'it probably does, I've been listening to his record all week.'

'Well,' he retorted, 'you can't play Bach like that.' I didn't know how he expected me to play him – so I quickly dropped the subject and tried to avoid it thereafter.

Both John and Millicent were mad keen on Bach; he was John's great idol. Some people live for certain things and John Francis lives for Bach. He would say to me, apropos of some Bach pieces, 'Jimmy, I want you to learn such-and-such.' I would protest: 'Listen, John, I don't like that music. I don't want to play it. I don't understand it and it doesn't mean anything to me.' At sixteen, I wanted to play Paganini, not Bach. He made this enormous effort to make me learn Bach's B Minor Sonata. Well, it's a hefty piece of cake, that one, and it really took me a bit of thinking to get round to doing it. Today, it gives me no trouble; in those days it was like climbing Everest for the first time.

Marcel Moyse, of course, remains my great idol. He has been the major influence on my style of playing. I remember when I returned to Belfast for a 'holiday' during my first year with John Francis, I did nothing else but practise the Moyse studies. I got so carried away that I hardly ever left the house and when I returned to London everybody wondered where on earth I had been and what sort of holiday I'd had; my face was as white as a sheet. But I returned twice as good a player as I had left and full of a sense of accomplishment and pleasure; a strange feeling that I was to know once again, only a short while ago, when I stood up in the class that Marcel Moyse conducts in an old church in Switzerland and played for him personally some of those old studies I had practised as a kid.

Despite the continuing shortage of money, I made it a habit to return to Belfast every summer and then, as time went by, to get home at Christmas as well. I worked only once in Belfast during these years when I was asked to play in a concert at the Ulster Hall with the City of Belfast Symphony Orchestra. This was at a performance of *Hansel and Gretel,* conducted by Maurice Miles.

Again, of course, I was hardly even into the house before I had the flute out and was belting away and giving the neighbours an excuse to complain to each other, 'There's Jim Galway again with that ould flute of his.' The trouble was that they couldn't sleep when I was at home and when I went away and there was no flute to annoy them, the sheer absence of noise made it impossible for them to sleep then either. My poor neighbours, they had to put up with a lot! But they were the most tolerant lot of people any kid could hope to live beside.

Meanwhile I was still playing away with the old flute my father had bought for me for £30. In London, however, I came across a beautiful instrument made by a famous French maker called Louis Lott, which somebody was willing to sell to me for £100. But they were having a bad time at No 17 Carnalea Street at that time and my dad was a bit short of the readies. He was in the middle of some argument with the unemployment people just then and was railing against them bitterly. So far as I can gather he had run out of dole benefit and they wanted to put him on Supplementary Benefit. But to an Ulster Protestant, you know, that's something like a red rag to a bull. The 'buroo' (a Belfast corruption of 'Unemployment Bureau') was all right, because by working and paying for your stamps, you had earned that. But he couldn't understand how anybody 'earned' Supplementary Benefit. To him it was just another word for charity.

So in desperation I took my problem up to the 39th Old Boys and they lent me the £100 to buy it.

I had ceased to play with the band by now of course, but I had not – and still have not – severed my connections. Each time I went home, I would go over to Billy Dunwoody's school on the Beersbridge Road and play a concert for the band. The band room always smells of smoke, of course; all the Belfast street bands seem to nurture this ambition to asphyxiate themselves. But it was a tremendous experience to stand up in front of all my old friends and belt out a considerable repertoire. On one occasion Jimmy McBride, the secretary, declared, 'You know, Jimmy, I'm getting more and more amazed. Every time you come home I tell you that you're getting better. But you *keep* getting better and better every time!'

It was truly marvellous that first time to be back again in Belfast and to see all my old mates. Everybody was very impressed, of course; I mean, living in a house with a fellow who owned a Rolls-Royce, just to begin with! But they were genuinely impressed and pleased with my success in obtaining the scholarship, although I myself had already become aware that I was undergoing that most awful of processes – growing away from them. Becoming one of that breed they call 'international Belfastmen'. I like to think that I have managed to avoid the worst excesses of this experience. Most of my old friends remain my old friends.

When I played with the Belfast Military Band, for instance, they staged dances every Saturday night in their band room at which my mother played the piano, Wee Dickie played the fiddle, George, my brother, played the clarinet, and somebody else the drums, and it was during one of these occasion that an old bachelor with the band, called Jimmy Miller, introduced me to two girls who played the piano very well. One of them was a girl called Etta Gault who has been ever since a dear friend of mine. Subsequently Etta and I used to go around Belfast playing flute-and-piano duets in old folks homes and places like that – churning out 'Home Sweet Home' and that sort of thing; we became so good, indeed, that we won a few competitions. Etta is now married to John Little, another close friend who also came from a musically inclined family. Although self-taught, he is a good pianist and singer and also plays the flute a bit. They were the first of my old friends ever to visit me in London. Now they have two kids of their own, one of whom plays the piano like a genius and the other who unquestionably plays the flute as well as I did at the same age – he's only four.

Yet that first visit home was overshadowed by a genuine

sorrow. My Aunt Sadie, my mother's sister, was dying of cancer at the time and I remember contrasting all the happiness and joy I was feeling at my success in London with the sad face lying on that pillow in that little terrace house in a Belfast back street. The moment seared itself into my mind. There was I with all the world opening out before me and there was somebody very dear to me and very dear to my mother, getting ready to die. Had I not had a religious bent then, I would most certainly have developed one.

It was with some relief, then, that I sailed away from Belfast and returned again to London and to my struggles to become a competent flautist.

CHAPTER EIGHT

Looking back now, I see that road as a long and arduous one because the fact is that you learn a lot of things from many people. You have to spend a lot of time and energy just picking people's brains and learning here and there, lifting this and that.

Listening to those records of Marcel Moyse I realized that there was a much deeper way of expressing oneself on the flute which had nothing to do with merely having good tone. It had something to do with the tone being very personal and you being the tone. It was really only when I began to study Moyse intensively, when I practised his scales and arpeggios incessantly, that my flute-playing improved by leaps and bounds.

William Bennett came into my life shortly after I went to live with John Francis. He was about three or four years older than I, and I thought he was just the bee's knees. He could play everything I couldn't at that time. He was a real flute maniac and whereas I might leave off long enough to eat a meal, William was such a zealot that he would, so to speak, try to cram a steak between his teeth while still making an *embouchure* on the flute. He had served in the Army for a while and was on every count pretty unorthodox. There was I, a good little boy from Belfast, no swearing, no drinking, no nothing, and there was William, a real man-of-the-world. At this time he was studying at the Guildhall with Geoffrey Gilbert.

Just round the corner in Marlborough Place, not very far from Lord Harewood's house (Galway had gone up in the world with a vengeance!) stood a synagogue. We students were always looking for some place to play in between our pea-pushing and nail-bending classes and so a small group of us eventually met there every Friday evening. There were three violins and a cello as well as William and me on the flute. The conductor was a very nice fellow called James Verity who played with the Morley College orchestra and who sported a Thomas Beecham beard – every aspiring musician sported a Thomas Beecham beard in those days. There weren't many Jewish flute-players around at the time, fortunately, so no objections were raised when William and I put in an appearance.

From our first meeting William had a great influence on me. I thought him a marvellous character and a great musician and he showed me a lot of things on the flute. He told me which pieces to practise to overcome certain difficulties. At that time I was really not very agile on the instrument. I couldn't do great slurs. I couldn't go easily in legato passages from one note to a higher note – at least not without a major operation. So William put me on to some exercises by Marcel Moyse designed to overcome this. Then he showed me some fingerings I should use – in those days I used some really weird ones. This, of course, is the kind of thing colleges ought to exist to put right, but some guys can't hear whether you've got the right fingering on D or not. And I hadn't. I had been shown the academically correct fingerings, of course, but there comes a point when you can depart from these and get away into something better.

I'd say, 'William, listen. I can't do this, you know. There's a certain thing I can't do – I can't play eight semiquavers in a two-four bar.' The first one was a rest and I was always late. So he demonstrated by playing the first few bars of the Ibert

Concerto. I gradually mastered this – although it kept me awake for some time. I have to repeat, however, that knowledge comes not only from one quarter. It was in the college itself that I finally solved the old problem that had first surfaced when I was being taught by my Uncle Joe; this problem of six-eight time. It was in a class taken by Archie Camden, the bassoon player. All went well until we came to Beethoven's Seventh Symphony, which has all these particular six-eight problems. 'Listen,' said Archie as the class got itself into a tangle, quite a lot of it due to one James Galway, 'this rhythm is really very easy. All you've got to do is sing "Amsterdam, Amsterdam, Amsterdam".' (To the end of my symphonic days I still hummed 'Amsterdam, Amsterdam, Amsterdam' when I played Beethoven's Seventh.) Then he went on: 'If you've got five to play, what you say is "hip-popotamus, hip-po-pot-a-mus,' etc.' That way you get five notes perfectly in time although, of course, it is necessary to get the conception itself firmly fixed in your head first.

There was yet another thing I couldn't do in those days. I could never start a note with the kind of *zip* or *ping* that I wanted. With a piano, for instance, you get this immediate *ping*! But to me the flute always sounded like *fou*! William showed me how to overcome this. He explained that he had just been to Paris. 'I know now how to do this, to *attack* a note on the flute. The term for it is *detaché*.' So he showed me how to do this elusive *detaché* and I discovered that there was really no particular trick involved. It just meant playing one note and putting your tongue really far forward and making it all sound like a bell from the beginning, really like a *bong-g-g*! So I practised this one note, going slowly down the flute until I got to the low note where it gets much more difficult. Anyhow, I just kept plugging away until I had really mastered the manoeuvre.

William and I knocked about together for many years. He was a really wild guy and great fun. I remember when he made his first seven quid, he took me out to a Greek restaurant in Soho and blew the lot. I can still recall that flat bread and that terrific kebab; for me, in those days, that was really high living. I felt I had already arrived. Not that I could have told you where.

He took me home to meet his parents on several occasions. His father, Frank, was a successful architect who was pretty certain that his son was wasting his time. One Sunday at the lunch table he turned to me and inquired, 'Tell me, James, do you really think you will ever make a living just blowing a flute? I sometimes wonder about William.' He could not understand why William and I should spend hours every day practising like lunatics so that we could one day join an orchestra. He would thump home the fact that only a handful of aspiring musicians ever get anywhere.

Later, it was William who told me about a job with Sadler's Wells Opera which I joined as second flute to his first. He remained a real hoot. Once when we were on tour, for instance, we got to Manchester, I think, and William said, 'Listen, Jimmy, you play the next three shows – I'm going off to collect some elder flowers.' What had happened was that he had spotted a clump of elder flowers – or maybe only a single elder flower – from the train. So off he went, backtracking along the railway line only to turn up again with five suitcases of the stuff. He then carefully emptied the contents into little bags which he sent home to his wife with instructions to make wine.

He continually looked for a chance to play a practical joke. Once we pinched some wigs from the wardrobe and walked out into the street wearing them. When we went into a restaurant, William took off the wig and hung it on a peg, startling the life out of half the customers. Then he dragged me into a chemist's shop and told the assistant that I'd had an electric shock which had turned my hair grey and was there any ointment or other treatment she could suggest to help me.

Everything he did was marked by a slight barminess. English concert halls are notoriously cold places – at least for the performers. So William took to carrying this blow-heater around with him. During the performance of a flute concerto in the Milton Hall, Manchester, everybody suddenly noticed this slight buzzing overlying the music. We worked our way through one movement before anybody discovered that it was William's blower at work and we got right through a second before they found out where he had plugged it in.

When it wasn't the blower that was distracting everybody, it was William's dog Jumble. Jumble was a perfect replica of the dog on the old HMV records – minus the old gramophone horn. To top everything he was stone deaf and would just stand and stare at us when we barked at him. The trouble was that William insisted on bringing Jumble onto the platform with him. The sight of a dog doing an imitation of the HMV dog generally unnerved the audience, some of whom became unhinged as they waited for Jumble to open his mouth and bark. The great composers have written-in parts for clocks and toys, but as yet we still await the masterpiece set to the theme of a barking dog.

Six feet tall, blond, good-looking, William now plays with the English Chamber Orchestra and has made a number of very fine records. To see and hear him play, it is impossible to imagine him as the perpetrator of the contretemps that suddenly hit Sadler's Wells Opera one night. A terrific stink of gas began to pervade the place, so with a nod to me to carry on, William stole stealthily from his place in the pit and disappeared round the side of the proscenium arch. At the end of the act, uproar struck the opera house. Somebody had dismantled a gas stove belonging to the stage-hands who hadn't had their tea break yet. Not only that, but some of the vital parts had been hidden. The entire interval was filled with roars and cries of recrimination and outrage, with William demanding that the offending gas stove remain dismantled and the stage-hands refusing to do any work until it was put together again and they had had their tea. The hassle between management, stage-hands, union officials, singers, musicians, scene-shifters, William and goodness knows who else overshadowed in theatricality anything that could have possibly happened subsequently on the stage itself.

All this still lay in the future, though. I was to remain in John Francis's house for three years altogether, learning and practising all the time. There were no set hours for practice. Just as soon as I got up and had had my breakfast each morning, then it was straight up the stairs and back to practice again.

Most of the time, John's house sounded like a music college. In the room opposite me was a pianist called Diana

Koshiden whose father, I understand, was Lord Chief Justice of Ghana. In another room was David Roth, the violinist, and John's daughter Sarah, who is my age, practised the oboe next door. Down below John himself played the flute and Millicent played the harpsichord. Later, their second daughter Hannah joined in on the harp. Occasionally, to top everything, the entire London Harpsichord Ensemble turned up and began rehearsals.

There is, of course, only one real way to become a good orchestral player – and that is to join or play with orchestras. So I became a member of the London Junior Orchestra and also had dates with the Morley College orchestra whose principal conductor was Lawrence Leonard, with Normal del Mar and Basil Cameron as guest conductors. What I principal conductor was Lawrence Leonard, with Norman often played in the Duke's Hall at the Royal Academy, which has this piece of oneupmanship on the Royal Albert Hall: Sir Thomas Beecham used to say of the latter (because of its notorious echo) that it was the only place in the world where a modern composer could hear his music *twice*. Well, in the Duke's Hall you heard everything at least four times – often five.

I enjoyed playing with the Morley College orchestra. Basil Cameron was a notable conductor; I thought he was terribly funny. Once when we were giving a performance of *Daphnis and Chloë*, he indirectly paid me one of the most extraordinary compliments I have ever received. There was too much noise in the hall while I was playing my solo, so Basil just lifted up a chair, flung it with a crash through a door and shouted, 'When you have such a wonderful flute-player as this, why don't you just listen to him!' You could have cut the silence with a knife.

Hoffnung played the tuba in this orchestra. To be honest, I don't know whether he could really play the tuba or not, but at least he didn't get in the way. One day during rehearsal, Lawrence stopped the orchestra and shouted, 'Hey, Gerry, I think that's an F sharp there you've got – but you're playing a B natural,' to which Gerry, feigning indignation, cracked us all up by declaring, 'Please don't talk to me like that because you'll really upset me as I'm a very sensitive artist, and then I won't be able to play at all.'

Many of the kids who played with me then made it big in the profession and are now playing with one or other of the major London orchestras.

I went on several courses during this period, which often posed difficulties because when you get a bunch of kids of varying abilities and instruments together, the results are not always worthwhile. But it did give me a chance to play with advanced string-players and I remember making my first trios for flute, violin and cello.

I suppose I have ricochetted about neither more nor less than most people who are determined to achieve a niche in life and have to take decisions or pursue courses of action that seem essential to the achievement of certain goals, even if they involve being a little unfair to others. At that time I was not ambitious in any real wordly sense. I was not after money or success or the plaudits of the crowd; I wasn't after them because they then lay beyond the scope of my vision, I simply hadn't got around to thinking like that. The limits of my ambition were to play the flute really well. I didn't want to be the Stanley Matthews or Pelé of the flute; I merely wished to play the instrument to the best of my ability and at that time I had no idea of the parameters of that ability. All I did know was that I had a heck of a lot to learn.

I still reckoned that, apart from the great figures like Marcel Moyse or Jean-Pierre Rampal with whose virtuosity I was only acquainted through records, Geoffrey Gilbert was the tops. I have heard it suggested that his virtuosity owes much to the French school but I don't believe this; I think his playing merely expresses his own personality and individuality.

What followed was painful for everybody concerned but time and a readiness to appreciate the reality of situations heal these bruises and friendships are restored. I had become restless and frustrated, conscious of the fact that if things had worked out differently I could have been Geoffrey Gilbert's pupil. On an impulse I rang him up and asked him if it were possible to receive lessons.

'I'm sorry, Galway, but it would be completely unethical

for me to teach you or even give you lessons while you are under tuition with John Francis.'

'Is there no way, then?'

'Only by resigning from the Royal College and leaving your present teacher, I'm afraid.'

The next few months proved traumatic, of course. I had to break the news to John Francis who had been so kind to me and to Millicent Silver who had been a second mother. I had to return to Belfast and, with the help of Douglas Dawn, arrange that my scholarship grant should be transferred from the Royal College to the Guildhall. I had to leave John's beautiful house with its glorious garden and move into a flat in Notting Hill with my friend Robert Dawes who played with the BBC Concert Orchestra.

I was still a pretty strange sort of kid, I suppose; a mixture of introversions and extroversions and still very much the product of my early environment. For instance, I preferred to practise on my own rather than with the other kids in college and I did not socialize much. They came from a different walk of life and I had a complex about this. It wasn't an important complex but it existed and produced a sense of uneasiness in my relations which I tried to avoid by walking away from the problem. First, there was the question of my religious upbringing; I was still very much influenced by Irish Protestant teaching. I could not understand all these kids drinking and messing around and getting involved with sex and therefore I was a bit shy. As a matter of fact, I was *very* shy – particularly with girls. And still am, believe it or not. It was a bit of a shock for me when I got to England and saw all these heathens drinking and all the rest of it so I never wanted to socialize in large groups, or go to parties. Once I accidentally found myself at a party. I had been rehearsing with a wind quartet and this friend of mind said, 'See you here next week at seven o'clock – right! Bit of a party, eh?' So I went along to the flat on time, expecting another rehearsal and thought it a bit funny that nobody had brought any instruments.

'Hey, is it all right if I go into another room and practise until everybody's here?'

'Sure, Jimmy, go ahead.'

So I disappeared into another room and had been practising for about an hour and a half all by myself when somebody walked in and said, 'Hey, Galway, aren't you coming to the party?'

I said, 'What party?'

'The party next door.'

'Isn't this a rehearsal?'

'No, you dope. It's a *party*. You know, people enjoying themselves. Chicks and that sort of thing.'

So I stuck my nose in the door and then, thoroughly scared, scooted off home.

There were other traumas that summer I left John Francis. Largest of them all, perhaps, was the fact that I fell in love.

Her name was Annabelle Lancaster and she played the flute and the piano and for a few weeks it was cloud nine. I got to know her by accident. I had telephoned a flat to talk to one of the girls I knew at college and Annabelle answered instead. So I invited her out for a beer and to my surprise we got on like a house on fire. She was my first introduction to girls as girls, if you know what I mean, and for the few weeks that the affair lasted, even my precious flute had to take second place. She invited me to meet her parents one weekend, so we went down to Stroud in Gloucestershire where her father, a company director, picked us up in his Jaguar – very impressive so far as I was concerned. Annabelle meant the whole world to me and we spent every moment we could together, just holding hands and mooning about. That summer I took a job in Bexhill, playing in the local Pavilion with an orchestra, but I was hardly ever off the telephone to Annabelle and I was back in London every weekend.

I had taken the job in Bexhill because I was fed-up with the flat in Notting Hill. It proved a happy decision and that summer will never fade from my memory. The weather was glorious, Bexhill pleasant, the people in the orchestra marvellous – and I was in love with Annabelle. On top of that I met a warm-hearted couple, Mr and Mrs Carter, who rented me a room for the season and whose kindness I can never really repay.

The first digs I moved into almost put me off Bexhill for life. The food was appalling, the landlady hated it when I practised and talked incessantly about her son who was some sort of a piano-player; she spoke of him as though he were Paderewski which, in the end, drove me up the wall. So I went for a walk, knocked on a couple of doors and eventually was directed to Mrs Carter who rented me the room and made me one of the family. Years later, when I had made my first solo recordings, she wrote me, 'Jimmy, if I'd known you were going to do something like this when you were living in my house, I wouldn't have complained so much when you were practising your scales.' To be frank, she had a lot to put up with – I nearly ripped my head off practising scales that summer.

We were quite a merry bunch in the orchestra; Daphne Webb on cello, Ruth Davis on viola, Brenda Cullity on violin, Clifford Bevin (who later played with the jazz group, the Temperance Seven) on trombone, Terry Leahy (who is now with the RPO) on trumpet and Harry Green on piano. One day we nicked a sign from a local restaurant saying 'Music by Muzak' and hung it on Harry's piano. Every time Harry hit the keys, the audience burst out laughing. Harry, of course, couldn't see the sign and wondered what on earth was wrong with the audience. I mean, he could play selections from *Showboat* (the staple of our repertoire) as well as the next fellow.

During the day, I often flew a box-kite on the beach. One day, Terry Leahy got hold of my best shirt (with the gold cufflinks still in it) and hung it on the box-kite which then shot up in the air so that half Sussex could see Jimmy Galway's shirt-tails snapping in the wind. I waited my chance and hung *his* trousers on the kite. Then I allowed the lot to swing half-way out to sea. 'Hey, hey!' yelled Terry. 'My week's wages are in the pocket!'

'Serve you right if you lose the lot!' I yelled back.

His protests were lost in the blowing wind and the gales of laughter from the other members of the orchestra.

Back in London the big problem was to find somewhere to live. As I have said I was tired of the place in Notting Hill. The room looked as if somebody had taken a junk shop and thrown all its contents in through the window. There were

1 (*Left to right*) me, my mother and my brother George

2 The Onward Flute Band, with me kneeling on the left

3 My grandfather

4 With my parents and brother

5 As a teenager

6 Being coached by John Francis in the early days

7 Colin Davis, taken at a Prom rehearsal in the Albert Hall

8 Herbert von Karajan and the Berlin Philharmonic, with me in the centre of the second row

9 Herbert von Karajan

10 Discussing a score with Daniel Barenboim

11 With Michael Emmerson

12 Marcel Moyse

13 Annie and me on our wedding day, 2 May 1972

14 With Cleo Laine, receiving a silver disc for *Showpieces*, 30 January 1978

15 Taking a Master Class for the TV series

16 In hospital after the accident which altered my life

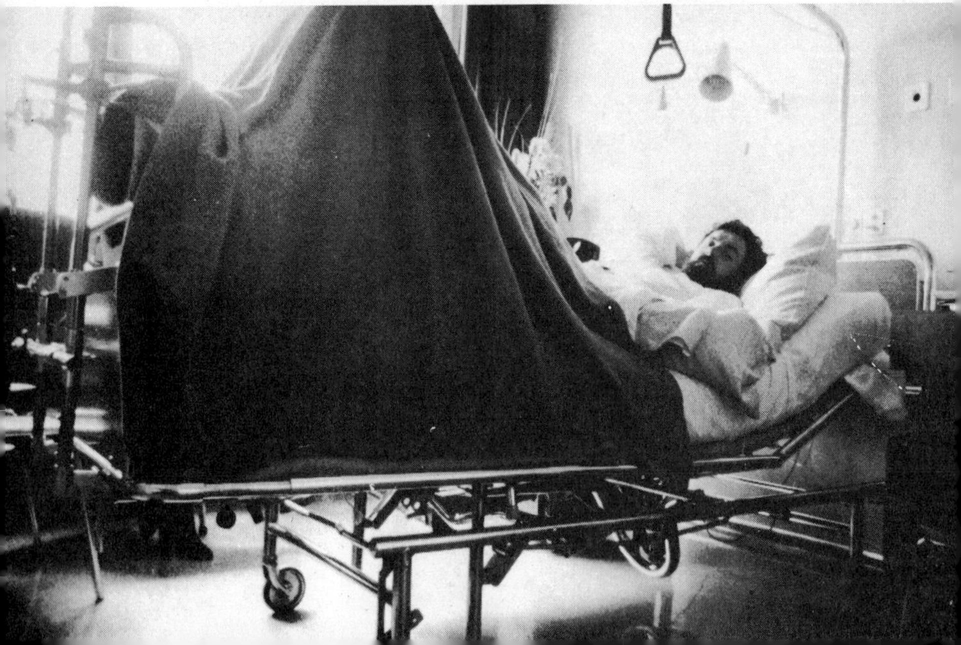

old bits of engines all over the place, motor spare parts and even a lathe in the small kitchen. The kitchen stank, partly from years of cooking spaghetti and onions and fish and chips, and from the oil from the lathe, which constantly ran all over the floor, and the landlady's cats which got in constantly. So, through the good offices of Nicholas Bush, who at that time was with the New Philharmonia, I found the most marvellous digs at No 211 Borough High Street.

I could scarcely have stumbled across a more engaging place. My landlady was called Jo Dodd and her house was the old jailer's house of what once was the Marshalsea Prison. Somebody had built a shop in front of this and to get to my room I had to walk up the side stairs to the shop, along a corridor, past the part where Jo lived, which had been the jailer's house, then up more flights to the attic where I was installed. This attic was where Little Dorrit was born. Charles Dickens, in fact, lived in the house while he wrote *Little Dorrit*.

My fellow lodgers were a couple of medical students and one or two nurses. Living there was a hoot – and even when I went off to Paris to study at the Conservatoire, I kept on my attic. Jo was as deaf as a post and could only hear through a hearing aid which she kept tucked away in her bosom; every time I wanted to speak to her, I had to lower my head and shout directly at her chest! Sometimes this left us both doubled up, the whole thing was so crazy. In the evenings, we held parties or played cards or practised music in her room which served equally as living room, dining-room and bedroom. Come eleven o'clock or so, Jo would go into the bathroom, undress there and come back and get into bed with a screen between us and her bed, switch off her hearing aid and leave us there to carouse away till morning if we wished. Night after night I would rip away on the flute while she slept soundly through it all. She had a keen sense of smell, however, and forbade us to smoke. It was about the only thing that was forbidden in that place.

One night when I was playing a gig somewhere, I decided to hitch-hike a ride home. A fairly swish car stopped and the driver offered me a lift as far as Trafalgar Square. I found him a most interesting man and, because of our animated conversation, he overshot the mark and we suddenly found ourselves heading south. I mentioned that I lived nearby and indicated a short cut so, with a laugh, he agreed to drop me outside the house where *Little Dorrit* had been written. When we got there, I asked him if he would like to see the room and maybe have a cup of coffee. I warned him that everybody would be asleep, however, and that we would have to take our shoes off and tiptoe up. So we negotiated all these flights and corridors successfully and I showed him into my attic which, on this occasion, made my old room in Notting Hill look, by comparison, something out of a Heal's catalogue. The bed was unmade, there was dirty linen all over the place, and there were bits and pieces of broken gramophones and tape recorders strewn everywhere else. 'Clear yourself a space and I'll make a cup of coffee,' I remarked nonchalantly. Then we sat and talked for a bit and I soon discovered he was very hot on politics, particularly African politics, and he expressed surprise that I had so little interest in the subject. He said his son lived in Rhodesia. When it was time to go, I took him downstairs and showed him which was north and which was south and how he could get to where he was going. 'It's very nice talking to you, Galway,' he said. 'If you ever get the chance, why not come round and see me?'

'OK,' I said. 'Where do you live?'

'Oh, call on me at the House of Lords,' he said. His name was Lord Stonham.

Next morning I told Jo. 'Hey, Jo – guess who was around here last night?'

'Who?'

'Lord Stonham.'

'James Galway,' she said slowly, 'I'll *murder* you. Bringing anybody into that place of yours is the next best thing to a crime. But to bring a lord. . . .' she was speechless.

I always meant to call on Lord Stonham. Then one day I read of his death and felt sad that I had not accepted his kind invitation. But that is the way much of my life has been – full of good intentions.

Suddenly the happy days were over and James Galway was plunged in the dumps. Annabelle had drifted away and I was inconsolable. I really lost heart for a while and for the first and only time in my life since I had first picked up a mouth-organ and penny-whistle, music ceased to mean anything to me. For weeks the flute lay there unplayed and I not once plucked a string of the guitar I was messing about with at the time. Instead, I painted. For the next month or so, I endeavoured to drown my sorrows in paint. Finally, however, I decided I would never make a painter. Technically I was good, but I soon realized I had nothing original to say. So it was back to the flute.

Two things helped to lift the depression and enabled me to bounce back. The first was a bunch of girls to whom I was introduced by my friend Robert Dawes; the second the start of my lessons with Geoffrey Gilbert and my tuition at the Guildhall.

There were these six chicks who shared a big flat in the Cromwell Road and who later moved into another somewhere in Earl's Court. They were a talented bunch of girls whom Bob eventually got around to calling my harem although, in fact, everything remained platonic. One was studying with John Francis, the others were a mixed bunch who attended the college and, I suppose, like any group of girls at that age, were all looking for husbands. Although I never thought of myself as husband material (at that time, anyway), Bob and I were made welcome and like any couple of red-blooded males made whatever mileage we could out of the situation. This generally involved bringing along the odd bottle of wine and joining the girls in a meal made for us with their own fair hands. After that it would be jokes, toots on the flute, records and what not. If I needed a kip for the night, there was always a rug on the floor. Two of the girls, Shelagh Melstrom and Kate Buchanan, once volunteered to cut my hair. I ought to have known better. When they had finished, all my dark curly locks lay on the floor and I sat there as bald as a Buddhist monk.

Marion Sprague was a flautist and I can still recall her beautiful brown eyes. Not that they were much good so far as I was concerned; she already had a boy friend who lived in John Francis's home. But we got on well together and she taught me to play chess. She and the others were a bit middle-class – everybody I met seemed to be middle-class or upper middle-class – and I remember one day I gave what I thought was a rather beautiful rendering of that Irish national glory variously known as 'O'Cahan's Lament', 'The Londonderry Air' or 'Danny Boy'. I think it is widely accepted that any country would be proud to possess this music. To my consternation and horror one of the girls shot out, 'Oh, Jimmy, that's such a kitschy tune.' The Lord alone knows what she expected from me in the relaxed mood of that particular moment – Beethoven's *Pathétique*, perhaps? Anyway, I felt hurt and *vaguely* disappointed.

My first lesson with Geoffrey Gilbert also left me feeling a little bruised and disappointed. I went along to his glorious house and was more than impressed by the splendour of his surroundings. He had an elaborate hi-fi system, a grand piano, an ornamented music-stand of obvious value, beautiful Japanese curtains and all his music and records so well organized in green boxes that the room had this feeling of distinction and orderliness. The first two pieces I played for him were the Prokofiev Sonata and the Hindemith. I really steamed through both and when I'd finished I stood there feeling pretty satisfied. I was also impressed by Geoffrey. He had accompanied me in both pieces on the piano, something rare for a professor specializing in another instrument. Then, while I was still busy preening myself, he shot a question at me. 'Tell me, Galway, do you play everything as loud as that?' Well, well, I thought, what's so loud about my playing? William Bennett, who was also his pupil, played at least as loud as I had. For a moment I was tempted to be cheeky, but discretion came to my rescue and I stammered out some innocuous reply which satisfied him for the moment.

Scales, techniques, enlargement of repertoire, these were the things in which Geoffrey Gilbert proceeded to coach me. I had many weaknesses to overcome in these days. I was in the car one day a short while before this with Lady Maude, wife of Sir John Maude, and a good friend at that time, and she said to me, 'You know, Jimmy, you should really practise the piano.'

'But I don't want to be a piano-player,' I objected. 'I want to play the flute.'

'You know,' she advised, 'you shouldn't put all your eggs in one basket.'

I couldn't explain to her that so far as I was concerned, I was not. She could not see inside my head where a little picture of that piano shop in Belfast still lurked. I had long ago decided that if the worst came to the worst, if I failed to make the grade, then it was back to wrecking pianos and I would be left to look back on my London experiences as part of a wonderful and protracted dream.

'But they insist you play the piano at college, don't they?' she continued.

'Yes, for some reason I don't understand, they do,' I admitted.

This was the sort of thing they *had* wanted me to do at the Royal College of Music. But I had stuck to my guns through thick and thin there, constantly evading the piano lessons, even avoiding the piano examinations although more than once threatened with the boot by the head of the College, Ernest Buck. Earlier John Francis had sent me to a lady called Margaret Hubicki for some private lessons in harmony and counterpoint, but my heart had not been in them because it had seemed to me then that the two or three hours a day I was spending swotting up theory could have been better spent training muscles which were then at a stage to be trained. You simply do not start training your muscles when you are twenty-five or six; that's too late. I argue that when you are young you should spend a very great deal of your time just moving your fingers about, just educating them to do a job and that you should not clutter up your head with a lot of facts you do not need and which are of no assistance in helping you actually to play. The most essential thing is to develop the feeling in your heart and not the matter in your head. Some of the greatest virtuosi, many of the great violinists for instance, have learned to play by playing, not by imbibing information.

Geoffrey Gilbert's great ability was to analyse the situation as it then stood for the student and to put his finger on exactly where the student was at. He always knew exactly where I was and how much to give me for the following week. Some teachers tell you the whole theory of the universe at one go. But a good teacher like Geoffrey can tell you, 'You're here, at such-and-such a point and for next week, I'd like you to do such-and-such and that will take us up to this point.' And gradually, over a period of a month or so, the whole programme would begin to unfold and I would find myself understanding.

I remember how he noticed that I was not very good on the top of the flute, on the high notes. So he gave me a study and when I opened it, I found that the first two pages were entirely made up of notes in the telegraph poles – that is, right above the line where the notes are written above the stave with all those little dots. After a month or two of such studies, my playing had improved enormously and I was good all over the flute. He also gave me his scale method to do and that improved me very much, too.

Trying to sum up exactly what I learned from John Francis and Geoffrey Gilbert is scarcely easy, particularly if by emphasising one aspect of my training I should be unconsciously doing an injustice to either of these fine men to whom I owe so much. From John I learned a way of life, a way of living which opened my eyes intellectually and culturally. He handed me the key to the theatre, to the world of the great thinkers and significant writers. I was a much more developed human being after I had been through John Francis's hands, no longer the raw, gauche lad from the back-streets. He helped me technically, too, in innumerable ways and his insistence that I swotted up orchestral excerpts for the flute later stood me in good stead when I auditioned for the Berlin Philharmonic. If he hadn't made me learn so many pieces so thoroughly from memory while I was still a kid, I would not have been able to display the confidence I did.

Geoffrey's forte was to teach me the flute really well. He helped to give me a style, a personal way of playing. He himself had a unique style, very expressive, a very extrovert way of playing reflecting the very extrovert kind of man he is in his quiet English way. He had a nice dry sense of humour. During this period, while I was studying at the Guildhall and taking lessons from him, I was already doing all sorts of little gigs here and there. One day somebody rang me up and asked me if I would do a gig in Manchester. I was due to take a lesson from Geoffrey, but I rang up his wife and said I had diarrhoea, a favourite excuse in those days with us students. The gig was to play second flute for the BBC Northern Orchestra and to my horror, just as we all settled into place, who should stride onto the platform to give a solo performance of the Nielsen Concerto, but Geoffrey. He took his bow, then turned to me and said, 'Oh, there you are, I thought you were ill?'

'I am, as a matter of fact,' I managed to stutter, wishing the floor would open under me.

'Well, you'd better come for your lesson tomorrow morning, don't you think?'

So not only did I have the pleasure of playing with the orchestra, but also of hearing him perform. Later I joined up with William Bennett, who was playing in Manchester at that time and he introduced me to one or two well-known players then working in the north. We spent the evening drinking beer and discussing the Halle and what it was like to play with Sir John Barbirolli and I ended up with this distant feeling that I was at last getting into the swim of things. Contact with Geoffrey helped me enormously psychologically. He had played with Beecham in the great days of the Royal Philharmonic and I had heard him playing with Jack Brymer, the great clarinettist, and Terence MacDonagh, the great oboe-player. Together as a trio they had set up new standards in England.

So far as the Guildhall itself was concerned, I don't think I really enjoyed it any more than I had enjoyed the Royal College. There were all sorts of things going on there that I simply did not attend, even though I was supposed to. The place, of course, was full of incipient actors and actresses attending the drama school and they put me off no end.

There were only two classes that I really enjoyed. One was the French lesson conducted by a marvellous lady called Madame Tasartey. She and I got on like a house on fire, mainly, I think, because neither of us ever quite understood what the other was saying. I would always turn up late – par for the Galway course – and would never have had anything to eat and she would inevitably ask, in her thick French accent, ' 'ave you had anyzing to eat this morning, Jeemy?' and I would answer in my equally thick Belfast accent, 'No, I haaven't haad aanything to eat,' and she would rummage in her handbag and produce a piece of bread or something and give me a nibble. Sometimes I would take a bite or two and she would stuff it away again in her handbag.

I also enjoyed the musical appreciation class, conducted by Ernest Newman who demonstrated his lectures with gramophone records. Almost everything else I gave a miss to and I don't remember playing the piano all the time I was at the Guildhall. So far as I was concerned, I wasn't planning to take over the world on the piano.

I never actually sought trouble, but it had this irritating habit of finding me. One day I discovered all the practice rooms full so I buried myself away in the toilet set aside for the professors and proceeded to rehearse for a forthcoming concert. One or two teachers came in and said the flute really sounded great in there. Then the head of the Guildhall turned up and I have never seen any man's face turn redder. Once before I had crossed his path. This was when he had acted as adjudicator at the Holywood (County Down) Festival where he had placed me second, saying that he didn't like the edition I used. Now he really was annoyed. What did I mean by practising in the toilet? Didn't I know there were practice rooms? What was I trying to do to the Guildhall? I stood there feeling like a revolutionary or something, vainly trying to point out that there were no practice rooms available.

On the whole, however, although I have little time for the music colleges as institutions designed to teach you how to play an instrument, I now tend to look back on my days at the Guildhall with some degree of affection and gratitude. The Guildhall helped to get me into the *feel* of the music world; I did pick up some useful tips; and, finally, I made some friends. Today I sometimes allow myself to see both the Royal College and the Guildhall through a haze of nostalgia. They were, after all, part of my youth. And therefore, as I now see it, part of the stuff of which dreams are made on.

CHAPTER NINE

The scholarship which had allowed me to spend a year with Geoffrey Gilbert was now coming to an end and it was time for me to move on. I had become, under the tutelage of two great teachers, a proficient flautist. But there were plenty of other proficient flautists about and I was scarcely at the stage yet when I could afford to sit back and rest on my laurels. This little matter of sustaining myself, too, had now begun to loom pressingly. Musicians and money are constantly argy-bargying with each other. There is never enough of the stuff about, particularly when you need it.

It was Geoffrey who suggested that I should investigate the possibilities of a grant to attend the Paris Conservatoire. The pre-eminence of French flautists has long been recognized and if I were ever to move out of the second division, so to speak, Paris seemed an essential bus-stop.

Luck was with me, for I had become friendly with Tony Mayer, cultural attaché to the French Embassy, who had heard me play. I went to see Tony, who lived in rather grandiose style in Eaton Square, and he told me that if I applied for a grant, he would see what could be done. Later he asked me round to his office. 'Look, Jimmy, do you really want to play the flute?' For some reason I have never been able to fathom, nobody ever wishes to push flute-players. Piano-players? – everybody wants to shower them with gold dust. 'Yes.' He looked thoughtful. 'You wouldn't like to be a conductor? Or something?'

The idea of me conducting a bus is preposterous enough; the idea of me conducting a full symphony orchestra sounded like science-fiction. 'Look, Tony. Having to learn all those scores and learn all that other stuff. . . .' I sought for words that would at once sound valid and yet not fail to portray me as a hard-working and serious musician. 'Besides,' I added heavily, 'I'm too small.' (On top of my other complexes, I had this thing about my height at that time. I seemed to be smaller than everybody else in the world. I kept thinking I was simply a tall midget. People reminded me that Napoleon had been only five feet one and that I would have towered over Schubert, but none of it made any difference.)

'OK, Jimmy,' he sighed, 'I'll arrange an audition for you.'

In the meantime, there was the rent to pay, so I landed a job with the Royal Shakespeare Theatre in Stratford-on-Avon. The new director then was Peter Hall who, years later, staged a recital for me in the National Theatre on the South Bank which proved a great success. Stratford, need I say, was an interesting experience. Among the actors I met there were Peter O'Toole, the late Max Adrian, Dorothy Tutin, the late Patrick Wymark, Dinsdale Landen and Jack MacGowran. One or two beers got downed during the process of getting to know each other, oddly enough.

One of my greatest friends at Stratford turned out to be Norman Archibald, later well known on the London orchestral scene. The big thing about Norman was that he owned a car and was always prepared to drive me about. The particular point about this favour is that I don't really travel well in a motor-car. Unlike other passengers who generally repay the kindness by telling jokes and keeping up the driver's morale in other little ways, I tend to treat a car like my mother's womb: a car to me is a place to doze in. Some time later when we were both in opera together, Norman picked me up at Little Dorrit's house and I managed to converse with him until we got as far as the bottom of the Edgware Road. When I woke up everybody was speaking with a Scottish accent and we were driving down Princes Street in Edinburgh.

Norman was a great guy and a very good influence so far as I was concerned. People used to complain of my practising, but Norman would say, 'Ignore them, Jimmy, just keep on practising your long notes. There's nothing like practising your long notes to get yourself a really good tone.' Every weekend we would both nip up to London in Norman's car, meet a few girls, have a drink at the Crown and Anchor overlooking Southwark Bridge and generally let off steam. Norman was a guy determined to get the last drop from life. He and I were always the last to leave the bar at night, the last two to go home from every party. But whatever we did, we were always on parade the next day.

It was while I was still at Stratford that I was asked to audition at the French Institute in South Kensington for the Conservatoire. Eventually I heard that I had been awarded a scholarship and immediately took off for London where Tony Mayer helped me to get organized. I was still only twenty-one and, apart from a short trip to Vienna with a junior orchestra while I was still at college, I really knew nothing about travelling abroad. I shall never forget Tony's kindness and generosity.

At that time I didn't have two pennies to rub together and I must have looked a sad sight in many ways. Certainly people seeing me traipsing about, entering this big house in Eaton Square with a curious little black box affair tucked under my arm, must have thought I was either a burglar or an anarchist. Tony took one look at me and sighed, 'Jim,' he said, 'You'll at least need a new jacket.' So what did he do but take me off to the West End and buy me a perfectly cut affair. Then he said, 'You've been working hard – and you've an even harder period ahead of you. So go on down to my house, La Carmegan, in the Vaucluse and have yourself a short holiday.' Nobody can persuade me that music doesn't bring out the real goodness and generosity in people.

The Paris Conservatoire has two classes – *classe d'étranger* and *classe Française*, the latter providing only *one* place for a foreigner every year. I had to audition to decide if I was good enough for the latter. Auditions do not normally scare me but this was a most impressive affair. There were fifty-seven of us all told, and they started by locking us in a great room, then ordering us to stand side by side in a row, with the immediate result that there was a dreadful row, enough at least to waken Vivaldi. Eventually there were solo items and I was called forward to do my bit.

For a moment or so, it was pure farce. I found the music stand too high so, before commencing to play Mozart, I twiddled with the knob and lowered it. I had scarcely raised my flute to my lips when Gaston Crunell, an old teacher at the Conservatoire, shuffled forward and put the stand up again. I looked at him in astigmatic astonishment, then very deliberately reached forward and lowered it again. I couldn't understand why the distinguished jury which included one of the world's foremost flute-players, Jean-Pierre Rampal, and two or three other luminaries, seemed to find this absolutely hilarious. Only when I began work in the school did I discover that the tradition of the place is that when your professor says 'jump', you jump and that if he says 'stand on your left foot' you stand on your left foot! Any-how, I didn't get the message – at any rate not then. So I just steamed through the Mozart and then followed with a French piece and, like Frank Sinatra, was able to boast I had done it my way. I was admitted to the *classe Française*.

In the end the Conservatoire was to prove the most substantial disappointment of my career. I was only twenty-one. I was desperately idealistic, looking for all the answers in a single word. And I was in Paris. And the word never came. Nor any of the answers, either. Within eight months I was ready to quit. And, in fact, I did quit.

Every young student sets out seeking something – seeking a message. He longs for a teacher who will place his hand on his head and change his life magically and instantaneously. At that time I believed that the nicest sort of flute-playing, the *virtuoso*, was to be found only in France. But what I wanted to know was *why* – and for the life of me, there was no way I could find out. Because nobody would tell me. In fact, I was to discover that it was what I was doing, practising eight hours every day, one day after the other, that makes you *virtuoso*. There was, quite unknown to me, also a kind of ambience coming in to assist me which I was totally unaware of, totally unable to appreciate. The secret, as I came to realize afterwards, was that at the Conservatoire lessons were never given privately. You had to play as a member of a class. You turned up, did your piece and then the next guy played the same piece – but faster. And the third guy played it even faster. If you happened to be guy number five or six, you were blowing up a real storm by the time it got your length. What this method did was to teach me to discover the nerve to play in front of other people, to really show what I could do. I had always been competitive, anyhow – I still am, in fact – so there was no difficulty there. My competitiveness thoroughly aroused, I played like a madman.

Not, as I say, that I had ever suffered much from nerves. The only occasion I can ever recall giving a performance and finding it marred by nerves was, as I have related, when I played as a kid in Belfast with Duggie Dawn in the Wellington Hall. Playing in the Conservatoire simply made me play harder than anybody else because I really wanted to show those guys. However, I was also busy, though I didn't realize it, conquering technique – going deep into scales, arpeggios, articulation – which would enable me, eventually, to play music properly.

At the time, though, ironically, I was sure I wasn't learning anything. My teacher had his own problems (the poor man had a tumour on the brain) but it seemed to me that there were better ways to employ my time than just standing there belting out a number while he hid behind his *France Soir* and smoked interminable Gauloises. I could stand in front of a guy like that anywhere; it didn't have to be in Paris. What I expected from him was instruction: 'Look, do it like this,' or 'This is the right way to do that.' But he just let each of us play our piece in turn while he studied the runners at Longchamps or whatever, and then barked, 'Right, next!.'

Not that I would describe Paris as a waste of time by any stretch of the imagination – although, as I've said, the Conservatoire seemed to be so then. One of the first guys I bumped into was a man called Martin Silver, a librarian from California who had come across to learn the flute. Through him I got to know a girl called Gail Grinstead, a French-speaking Canadian who had the most bizarre command of the English language. On any count she was one of the nicest girls I have ever met but somebody had played a bit of a joke on her and her English consisted of a string of swear words, really strong stuff. Speaking French she never as much as said, '*Mon Dieu!*'. When she essayed English, however, it was worse than the language used in the barrack room of a parachute brigade. It would have been a major task to teach her English properly, she was so far gone, and to the best of my knowledge she has continued to go through life effing and blinding in English, under the impression that this is the way they speak in Buckingham Palace.

'You know she's a pupil of Rampal's,' said Martin one day.

'Hey, really?' The Galway brain cells became galvanized. 'Listen, could I get lessons?'

'We can only find out.'

Through the good offices of Gail, therefore, it was arranged that I should have a few private lessons from the master. For me, of course, it was simply a sensation to meet this great musician; like a fiddler meeting Heifetz. He lived on the Avenue Mozart and there was a little baker's shop on the corner called La Flûte Enchantée.

'Why do you want to come here?' Rampal asked me after I had played a piece for him.

'I want to play in the French style, Maestro.'

'But you already play in the French style. Better than any Frenchman.'

Rampal was very nice and charming, but he neither taught nor advised me. What he did, instead, was *inspire* me. He did, of course, show me how to play the odd piece, but this was minor stuff compared with the real effect he had on me. He took me to several concerts and also to the Paris Opera where he often played. As I sat there in the sumptuous surroundings of perhaps the grandest opera house in the world, listening to Rampal, I knew an entirely new plane of experience.

When I began to get feedback from the Conservatoire for skipping lessons, he did his best to put me straight. 'Listen, Jimmy you've got to go to lessons here, you know.'

'But they're such a waste of time,' I objected.

'Yes, I know,' he humoured me. 'But you've got to do it.'

Instead, I soaked up the wonderful atmosphere of Paris. I delved into every museum and art gallery, mooched about Sainte Chappelle with my mind blown, spent more time in the Louvre than in the Conservatoire. Had I not been a flute-player, I suppose I would have wanted to be a painter more than anything else. I stared at some of the Louvre paintings so intently, particularly da Vinci's *Mona Lisa* and Delacroix's painting of Chopin, that they still remain in my memory like photographs. But I was in love with the whole of Paris, particularly its aromatic smells.

I stayed in the Cité de l'Université, on the south side, where they take all the students and lock them all up as far as possible out of harm's way. There are 'houses' there for students of all nationalities. There is a Japanese house, a Canadian house, a Brazilian house (built by Corbusier), a Spanish house and so on. I put up at the Franco-Britannique, easily the drabbest and worst-run house of them all; run by the British, of course. Everybody in the Spanish house was having a riot while the French-French house – la Maison de Provence de France – was like one big party.

Meantime, I practised and practised and when I wasn't practising, I was picking up the odd bob or two busking in the Metro. A bunch of us were among the first students ever to invade the Underground in this way and you can't really believe the kind of stuff we used to play down there. I played arias from *The Magic Flute* and other good stuff while the francs clattered into our bowl. One day a woman stopped and listened for a moment before saying to me, 'You know, you should take up music professionally.'

It could well be that Geoffrey Gilbert's painstaking tuition had spoiled me for the Paris Conservatoire. It could also be that my good staunch Protestant upbringing, with its inbred work ethic, also let me down. But at the time I simply could not understand what the Conservatoire was all about. Geoffrey, to my mind, had always been right on the ball, telling me exactly how to do everything so that I really knew what I was doing. The apparent lack of attention, the apparent lack of tuition, really upset me and one day, exasperated beyond all measure, I simply told my professor where he could go. The result was uproar and I had to go before a board representing the body who had awarded me the grant.

'Look, what are we going to do?' someone asked. 'Nothing,' I replied. 'There's nothing you can do. I'm going to leave. It's worse than useless here. I'm not learning anything.'

'People don't leave the Conservatoire. People don't walk out on scholarships. Look, couldn't you just claim you were sick – and go and learn with somebody else?'

'No, I'm not sick. I haven't been sick. I don't want to say I was sick. I've had enough of all this. I just want to leave and get a job.'

'We gave you a scholarship. We expect you to honour that obligation.'

'You can always give the money to somebody else. I'm fed up. I can't go on wasting time. Please accept my resignation.' There was nothing anybody could do, of course, and so I left Paris.

I am older and wiser now and recognize that my relatively brief stay in the French capital made me a very much better flute-player than I would otherwise have become. There is a marked difference between the methods practised by the Conservatoire and the British academies. To begin with, competition is the life-blood of the Paris system. When you also take into account that the standard of playing among the students is usually much higher, the value of that competition can perhaps be better appreciated. Kids flock from all over the globe to the Conservatoire so that the competition you face is truly international. I wasn't just competing with a bunch of British kids; I was taking on the best in the world. I am amazed now when I think back on the brilliance of my contemporaries there. The majority of them today occupy some of the top positions in European orchestral music; top flute with the French National Orchestra, first and second flutes with the Paris orchestra, first flutes in Hamburg, Geneva and other places.

The squeeze throughout is on the technical side with an emphasis that technique should be used primarily to produce beauty. In the final analysis, beauty, I suppose, is the key word. The French demand beauty; you must get the *sound* of the phrase right. In England, on the other hand, the emphasis, it seems to me, is on efficiency. Get this bit loud, this bit soft and so on. The idea that the sound you produce on the flute should seem *beautiful* only crops up more or less *en passant*.

One particular point that in retrospect appeals to me greatly is the Conservatoire's method of holding a *premier prix* competition at the end of term. Students are presented with a piece specially written by a French composer. As it is always a new piece, everybody starts level. The rivalry is intense and this leads to all-round excellence.

With the Conservatoire behind me and my funds cut off, I badly needed a job. Luckily I heard of one going with Sadler's Wells back in London where my old friend William Bennett was then playing first flute. The audition was conducted by Alexander Gibson (now Sir Alexander), John Ludlow, then leader, and one of the administrators. I was asked to do a sight reading.

Nobody, of course, ever does a *true* sight-reading. Professional musicians swot up all the different bits in the operatic repertoire and hope that they will be asked to play something they know. I struck it rich; a bit of *Carmen.* I waltzed through that. Then a few more bits and I could have been blind and still have got away with it.

Alex Gibson is nobody's fool, however. He studied me keenly, then walked over to the piano and played some fifths which sounded like the typical drone of a bagpipe. 'If I were to play this, what would you play on top of it, Jimmy?' he asked. I thought quickly, then broke into an Irish jig. Alex laughed and rose from the piano. 'OK, Jimmy, you've got the job.'

Nevertheless, I faced an acute personal problem. It was now May and the job didn't start until August. How, in the meantime, was I to live? Obviously I had to take a job – any job.

Have you ever tried for 'any' job? Just any old thing that would pay the rent and allow you a crust. Nothing taxing. Just something a man without eyes, ears, legs or arms could do? It is, believe it or not, almost impossible to find one. I applied for a job as a packer. That was all there was to it;

wrapping up parcels in brown paper and putting an address on them. I nearly fell over myself when I heard the size of the wage they were offering. I was bowled sideways when they *turned me down*! 'Oh, no, we need an experienced man,' I was told. A puling infant could have handled the job. Obviously they were looking for zombies, not somebody who gave the faint impression that he was capable of thinking.

Eventually, though, I landed a job in a nut-and-bolt factory; a real funny place. I started off on the second floor working with one other guy. 'You take this order,' he explained. 'This fellow wants twenty-five nuts and bolts, half-inch diameter. So just count out twenty-five – it ought to be easy for you because they're very big anyway – put them in a sack and address a label. OK?'

'OK,' I said.

He went away and I counted out twenty-five nuts and bolts, shoved them in a sack, addressed the label and then sat down and began reading the paper. Half an hour later this fellow turns up again. 'How did you get on?'

'Oh, I finished the lot.'

'What?' You could have heard his roar a mile away. 'Listen, Galway, never do that again! Don't work so quick! Slow it down, man, that's an order! Otherwise, the bosses will have you at it all day.'

I thought this just great, of course; it's marvellous to be paid for doing nothing. So the two of us used to sit there and wait for mice to appear and then sling nuts and bolts at them. In the end I got so bored that I went back to my original system of doing whatever had to be done within a couple of minutes and then sitting down to read *The Times* from cover to cover. One day, however, came the big announcement, 'Jimmy, you're fired! From now on, you're the lift-boy.' The regular lift-boy – described to me as someone who looked half-way between Frankenstein's monster and Dracula – had gone on holiday and I was to be his stand-in. When the guy eventually returned, I discovered the description apt enough; he stood about six feet ten inches tall and even his boots were almost as big as I was. Anyhow, for a fortnight I performed the duties of lift-boy. It soon occurred to me that all the work I was needed for could be crammed into the space of perhaps ten minutes. So I began taking the lift up to the top of the building, exiting through the emergency door onto the roof where I would lie down in the sun and read a book. Meanwhile, below me, all these guys were running around like crazy wondering where the lift had got to. I would hang about up on the roof for an hour, perhaps, then get back into the lift, shoot up and down in it like a maniac for maybe five or ten minutes or so, shifting all the bodies and all the goods that really needed shifting, then disappear out on the roof again for another hour or so before returning to operate the lift again. In this way, I managed to read the whole of *David Copperfield* and umpteen editions of *The Times*. Then I was sent back to the nuts and bolts department. 'I want two hundred of these,' somebody would say and I would count them out. 'I want a half-pound of these,' somebody else would ask and I would carefully weigh them. The whole thing became mind-boggling. Apart from which I became so tired from counting nuts and bolts and holding up heavy copies of *The Times* that I no longer had the strength to play the flute. To top everything I smelled constantly of axle-grease.

I don't think I have ever been so bored in my life. But the weeks were slipping by and August was almost upon me. It was time, fortunately, to return to a world of sane men, a world where there were things that it made some sort of sense to do.

CHAPTER TEN

Shortly after I joined Sadler's Wells, my good friend Alex Gibson moved on and a man whom I regard as one of England's chief glories. Colin Davis, became music director. Today, Colin Davis stands among the most eminent of the world's conductors and it is only when you see and hear the rapturous welcome given his performances by the Germans, for instance, that you begin to appreciate what a treasure Britain has and which it still, sadly, vaguely underestimates.

When Colin began conducting the Sadler's Wells orchestra, it was really remarkable how he made us play. We played with an expression which we never got with any other conductor, even Alex Gibson. With Alex gone, I think, there was a tendency for everybody to feel that they could take life a little easier, lapse into a comfortable routine, perhaps. The violins played in order to get through the thing and never bothered to play *vibrato*, for instance, being content just to sit there, play the note and not get involved any further. One day, shortly after his arrival, Colin rapped the stand and delivered a little speech. 'Look here,' he told us, 'why don't you play this phrase with truth and meaning?' Now that was a pretty big thing for a conductor to do. He wasn't simply instructing the orchestra how to play a piece; he was telling us to get our fingers out. In the event, his version of Mozart's *Idomeneo* proved so fantastic that I just sat enraptured through it. And no matter how many times we played it, I still thought it marvellous.

Karajan maintains that working with musicians in opera houses these days is a dead loss and that is why he becomes so involved in his Salzburg performances where he can train singers to do exactly what he wants and extract performances which are significantly his own. Much the same thing happened at Sadler's Wells with Colin. Hours were spent rehearsing orchestra and singers until he got it together exactly as he had conceived it. When I went to the Royal Opera in Covent Garden many famed conductors played with us but it seemed to me that much of what they did was mere theatre. We played just as we always played, belting out pieces as though they were all 'Old Comrades' or 'Abide with Me' and then going home as if we had spent the evening frying fish and chips. It was rare to find a conductor who had real contact with the orchestra or respect for the people in it, or who could provide the antagonism, the spark, to make them do something special together. There was a great sense of freedom about Colin's *Carmen* for instance. Philip Jones on oboe, Tom Kelly on clarinet, Tony Randall on horn – we were all together as a team and over the whole season we played the pants off *Carmen*; Colin simply lifted us and made everything take off.

He also had this sensitive feeling for our environment; even our personal appearance. He appreciated that personal sloppiness could spill over into sloppy performances. 'Now, look here,' he once addressed us, 'it's time, I think, we stopped being so lax about things. For example, members of the orchestra turn up unshaven. They look sloppy and think sloppy. I think it's time everybody made up their minds to present themselves at their best.' I understood what he was getting at. I know an old lady in Belfast who is seventy-five, yet if she only goes to buy some potatoes in the morning, she puts on her earrings and good hat and manages to look terrific and everybody feels better for meeting her. What Colin was driving at was that the orchestra should attempt to get rid of the stigma that attaches to most musicians – that they are a drunken, disorderly, unreliable bunch. He really galvanized us and from then on we became as punctual and orderly as a parade of Guards. Or very nearly.

Regrettably we lost one or two perks. Colin put a stop to the deputy system, so the opera job became a bit tight. What happened was that one night a guest conductor told us he would give us 'two bars in', meaning he would conduct two bars before anybody played. Unfortunately, the tuba-player sent down a deputy that evening who hadn't heard about this instruction and who began belting out the first two bars before anybody else started. Worse, once the tuba-player opened up, the curtain was raised so that the whole thing became a tremendous foul-up. This ended the system – an action much resented by the orchestra, of course. Musicians find much pleasure, and also make a bit more on the side by taking little jobs here, there and everywhere. In this way they are spared some of the monotony of going down to the same place every night and playing the same piece over and over again. In the end, it was this restriction on my freedom that led me to leave Sadler's Wells for a time, although when Colin himself left the whole bottom fell out of everything anyway.

Colin Davis, of course, represents one of a new breed of conductors. He is, to begin with, not an autocrat and does not subscribe to the iron-fisted tradition epitomized by Furtwangler, Karl Boehm and Karajan, which he regards as old-fashioned. He believes music today is going in a different direction and I share this view.

He is also a democrat. One day when I was really down in the dumps, kind of moody as I often was – and still often am – I was standing in a queue during the lunch break when Colin walked up beside me. 'What's the matter, Jimmy? You look really down today.'

'Yes,' I replied. 'But I don't know why.'

'All right,' he said. 'Why don't you have a good scream or something and get it all out of your system, eh?'

I had never screamed much, so how he got on to this, I'll

never know. 'What do you mean, "have a good scream"? It's not as simple as that you know.'

'Just shout and bawl at me – *right now*!' he insisted

So I stood there in the middle of the canteen and let a string of abuse really rip. You never heard such a load of insults and all delivered at top pitch. Colin seemed absolutely cracked up by it all and nearly laughed his head off. But the amazing thing was that the trick worked and I felt great afterwards.

Leaving aside such artistic and psychological problems, I have to say that the life of a musician is no great shakes on a purely physical level, either. For instance when I first joined Sadler's Wells, the pay was a princely £21 a week (this was before inflation really got started). When we toured we got an extra £7 a week maintenance – which was supposed to pay for our flat in London and our digs wherever we found ourselves. Conditions in the various theatres were diabolically primitive. There was never anywhere to hang a coat, for instance; not that anybody would have dreamed of leaving a coat on a peg, for everything that wasn't nailed down was nicked. In the main, British opera houses are like dustbins backstage. And so cold that the wonder is that we don't all die of pneumonia nightly. Even at Sadler's Wells there was a constant draught in the pit and although they rebuilt the area, it made no perceptible difference while I was there. The toilets, too, had to be seen to be believed. When anybody ever says to me, 'Oh, I'd like my kid to get into the music profession', I tell them to go and have a look at some of our opera houses first.

Managements, too, are often very cunning. We got paid by 'the call'. After so many calls in a week, you got paid overtime. That, at least, was the theory. But we had three flutes at Sadler's Wells and by swapping us around, the management regularly ensured that we did rehearsal after rehearsal and show after show without ever running into overtime. I can understand their worries about money, of course (not that we didn't have ours, too). Still there was no real excuse for their reluctance to allow us time off. For example, in January I might ask if I could have some time off in March or April. 'I'm sorry, Jimmy, but we don't know which opera we will be doing then,' would be the reply.

William Bennett, for one, got cheesed off by all this. To be fair, Bill had already set his sights on a career as a soloist. In pursuit of his goal he once asked for a day off which was refused.

'*Faust* is a very important opera for the flute,' the management told him. This was a totally absurd objection because the third flute at that time was Arthur Swanson who knew all the operas inside out and backwards – a lot better than most of the people who were invited to conduct us – and was a most capable player, anyway. But because of 'politics' (there was some sort of niggle going on between him and one of the senior members of the orchestra) the management refused to allow him to take over for the night. Bill was told that if he insisted on taking the date off, he need never come back. So he never did come back, and I found myself first flute.

I wasn't really quite ready for this job. I am not talking about my ability or technique, but simply about my psychological make-up. The whole idea of playing first flute at the Wells seemed so exciting – and my elevation so rapid and unexpected – that the old complex began to show itself. To start with there were all these fantastic names taking part – such as Peter Glossop, who later sang many times with Karajan in Salzburg, June Bronhill, Ronald Dowd, William McAlpine and, of course, the famous 'Flying Dutchman', David Ward. It was all such a glowing, magical ambience that I found I couldn't concentrate properly and sometimes I would come in wrong and the other guys in the orchestra would laugh at me.

Philip Jones once said, 'Listen, Jimmy, if you play this opera the whole way through tonight without doing anything wrong, I'll buy you a glass of beer.' Sometimes I would try and sometimes I would succeed – and if you're out there and listening, Philip, let me remind you I'm still waiting for those beers to materialize! The truth was that often I just wandered off and fell into a dream (it was like being back at Mountcollyer again). Hearing some of the great operatic arias played marvellously for the first time also made an enormous impression on me. For instance, when we played

Traviata, I could scarcely play a note because I was so enraptured. And Sadler's Wells weren't exactly employing me to *listen* to the music.

If the management often felt frustrated with me, I felt equally frustrated because of the tight discipline imposed on us. I even turned grumpy with Colin on occasions because I could not get time off to play my chamber-music gigs. Even in those days, I resented the anonymity of orchestral work and dreamed of a day when I would play solo. Orchestras might pay money but it was the gigs that provided the spiritual and psychological sustenance. After four years with Sadler's Wells, I decided to try my luck with the Royal Opera at Covent Garden, hoping to find myself more freedom.

It was an experience, alas, I could well have done without. The truth was that I did not possess the right routines to do that particular job, although, speaking quite objectively, I could play the flute better than anybody else there. What I needed at the time was a dose of good advice and assistance. Instead, what I got from the management was a complete lack of understanding. There was one man in particular who never gave me a chance to enlarge my experience and insisted on putting me on second flute although I had been engaged as first. I eventually got so frustrated that one day I went to see him and said, 'Look here, my contract here is to play first flute. I'm not going to spend all my time playing second.' He gazed at me coldly and then said, 'If you don't like it, you can leave.' My dander up, I said 'OK, I will.'

Through a piece of incredible luck, Colin Davis had just reformed the wind section at Sadler's Wells with Derek Wickens (now first oboe with the Royal Philharmonic), Alan Hammond (now bassoon with the RPO) and Roy Jowett (now co-principal clarinettist with the London Symphony Orchestra). I was offered – and took – my old job back, and from then on had a mighty fine time because we all agreed musically together and our personalities harmonized.

Doing the same thing night after night is not actually as boring as it sounds. The only exception so far as I'm concerned is Wagner – although when Colin did *The Flying Dutchman* I listened with new ears. But with Mister Wagner

I often wander into the land of nod; I once actually fell asleep when Colin was conducting the great Richard. That really is no insult to Colin for when I visited Vienna as a student with a junior orchestra, we were taken to hear von Karajan conduct *Rhinegold* and after the first few bars I went out like a light and only woke up when the performance was over. It happened again with Karajan when I went to hear a rehearsal at Salzburg. So I can really recommend Wagner to anybody who suffers from insomnia. Just put on your tape recorder and play two Wagner operas one after the other and you will find it better than Mogadon. Certainly Wagner is a genius to my way of thinking, but there are an awful lot of geniuses who don't make any difference to my life.

Well, concentration did prove a problem at times but it was possible to relax during performances which, in the end, often helped. Edwin Roxborough and I enjoyed our little bits of fun together. Edwin was not only a very good oboe-player but an excellent composer. Later, when I entered the International Woodwind Competition in Birmingham, I said to Edwin, 'Hey, Eddie, I'm going to do this competition next week and I don't have any cadenzas for the Mozart G Major. How about writing me some cadenzas?' So, literally four days before the competition began, he handed me these cadenzas which he had specially written. They were remarkably fine and helped me to win the competition; all the more remarkable in that he must have just sat down and scribbled them out. I still play them and even recorded them with Baumgartner and the Lucerne Festival Strings.

Eddie and I also played a game of musical chicken. I would say, 'OK, let's close the music and see how far we can get through this opera without opening it.' It was like the kind of thing I did as a kid in Carnalea Street when a bunch of us would see how near the railway line we could lay our heads without getting them chopped off. I even played chess with a Hungarian friend of mine during performances. We had a chess board beside us and made the moves when our parts were silent.

One of the guest conductors whom I much admired was Mario Bernardi whose *Traviata* was one of the finest I have ever heard. My first big recording session was for his *Hansel and Gretel*. This was one of the most exciting recording sessions of my life for we did it at the EMI studios in Abbey Road where the Beatles had made their albums. I was really in awe of the technical guys in those days and when I walked into the Abbey Road studios and recalled that these men had recorded artists like Maria Callas, every complex I ever had suddenly surfaced.

I often got mad, even lost my temper, with Colin Davis. He was an extremely understanding and sympathetic fellow, however, and knew pretty well how to handle me. One day he arrived on my doorstep. 'What are you doing, Jimmy?' he inquired.

'Nothing,' I said, wondering what this was all about.

'Right, come along then and have a curry.' So we dawdled off to a restaurant somewhere where we ate Bombay duck or something and chewed over the fat in that other sense.

There was something inside me in those days desperately trying to get out. I was never really mad at Colin; I was mad at my whole situation. Orchestral work did not really interest me. At that time, too, there seemed to be a view that flute music was rather inferior, a view, I think, which has begun to change. I liked Colin – I still like him. But I had this terrible temper – which unfortunately I still possess but which I hope I have learned to control better. I would get mad at people for no apparent reason and my mood might last for days. I don't know why I get mad like this except that when I do there is no talking to me, no reasoning with me. I am straightforward and I speak my mind and I have no capacity for dissimulation. In many respects this is a Belfast trait, I think. I have never learned to cover up my feelings.

What proved particularly irritating – and it still irritates me to some extent – is that while you are playing with an orchestra nobody will take seriously any ambition you may have to play solo. People treat you as if you were a lunatic when you talk about solo performance, or attempt to humour you as if you were a child.

I often boiled over, therefore, even with such a tremendous man as Colin Davis. One day there was a little flute solo somewhere and it didn't sound so good, so Colin called out,

'Hey, Jimmy, see that note on your flute, that's not the best note, is it?' Instead of accepting the reprimand meekly, I told Colin to mind his own business! He knew a lot about the instruments and he knew that I had played a bad note and that I was having trouble making the piece sound nice. Even today, you know, if I get up and I am not in the best of moods and somebody comes along and tells me that I'm not really up to scratch, that doesn't make me feel better; it makes me worse. That is really the sort of thing Colin and I used to have these little troubles about. And there is no question but that I often set out to annoy him deliberately. We were playing the National Anthem in Glasgow on one occasion. I was less than two feet away from him, right in front of him, so near that he could reach out and touch me. As he glanced down at me, I suddenly crossed my eyes at him. So the next time he brought the baton down, he leaned forward slightly and whacked it down much more sharply than usual, rapping me across the knuckles.

I have referred to these chamber-music gigs and perhaps it is as well to explain their appeal. It is a great thing when you don't need anyone to direct you and when a bunch of you can just agree among yourselves, then get onto a concert platform and somehow make the music all sound as though it were merely one person talking. I think the pop stars who play together in groups must experience the same sort of satisfaction. And the music itself is so tremendous. Mozart's Quartet for Flute; the Mendelssohn Octet, the Mozart Clarinet Quintet, the Schubert Octet, or the 'Trout' Quintet. Money is the last thing that you think of, then. It is your *spirit* that is involved.

Certainly money was never far from my thoughts in those days. I expended a great deal of time and effort trying to pick up an extra 12/6 a week (salaries were about £36 a week at that time) by playing a piccolo. A great deal of insecurity surrounds a musician's life – just as it does the theatrical profession. The Sadler's Wells management were shrewd enough to pick up on this and use it to their advantage. The trouble is, of course, that in the end the worm turns. The process is a fairly normal one, particularly if you are working in one of the creative or interpretative fields. But on top of these, I had all the normal worries related to my own personality. At the time I thought of these difficulties as peculiar only to me; wisdom and experience, naturally, have taught me that such things are universal. I was worried about my relationships with other people; my quick temper; my working-class hang-ups in a predominantly middle-class world. And then I was aware of the success other men around me appeared to be having with the opposite sex. There was a lot of crumpet around in the *corps de ballet*, none of which I ever succeeded in getting off with – although when I look back, I see that as the least of my worries. But at the time, when I saw these other guys going about with these various girls, it depressed me.

Looking back over my time at Covent Garden and Sadler's Wells, I cannot point to any one specific thing which helped me. It is almost impossible to pinpoint these things. Obviously the two experiences were crucial. I ceased to be a student and became a real professional musician – not that the process of learning ever ceases. I would like to have stayed at Covent Garden longer than I did. I made many good friends there and the sight of the curtain rising with 'the Queen's insignia' always gave me a thrill. Everything was done on such a grand scale. Great singers, great directors, distinguished audiences and spectacular performances, such as *Aida* when I think they were hauling people in off the street just to make up the hundreds of extras needed.

The Covent Garden orchestra was really fine, too; except when they had to play ballet. We all hated this and I think the orchestra's performance of *Les Sylphides* was the worst I have ever heard. Nonetheless if it had not been for this one person in the management who made my life miserable, I would have been content to become a permanent fixture at Covent Garden, or at least to the degree that I would ever want to make myself a permanent fixture anywhere.

Everything, however, comes to him who waits. A year or so later I bumped into the same guy on the steps of the Royal College of Music. 'Oh, hello, Jimmy. So what are you up to these days, then?'

'I've just finished with the BBC Symphony Orchestra,' I

said. I'll swear there was a look of quiet satisfaction on his face. Galway, obviously, hadn't made it. 'Yes,' I added, 'It's my last day with them. I've just signed a contract with the LSO.' Before he could recover from the blow, I really put the boot in. 'As first flute, of course,' I said.

CHAPTER ELEVEN

Eventually I moved away from my bohemian attic in the Borough and into another similar joint just behind the BBC, which I shared with one of my chums in the Sadler's Wells orchestra. When we first moved in the place was overrun with bugs and we had to get the local exterminator in. After a while, the arrangement fell apart, mainly because the place was too small for us to entertain girl friends satisfactorily. So I moved out and ended up in a small flat in Emperor's Gate, found for me by a friend, Naomi Davidoff, who lived in the next room.

Naomi played the piano and so we formed a little group with John Barnett who played the oboe at Covent Garden. We did little jobs here and there, playing at weddings or at churches in the city. We once did a church concert which was so badly publicized that only five people turned up as audience. John thought this such a hoot that he invited the entire audience to lunch.

My relationship with Naomi was strictly platonic – indeed, I had already met my first wife by this time – and although we had an enjoyable time (she made the most wonderful coffee and her salad and borscht dinners were superb) I had to move into a bigger place once I got married.

I had been playing *The Mikado* at Stratford when an old Paris friend of mine rang up and said he had these two French girls in tow and would I like to join them all for a drink. Claire LeBastard turned out to be small, dark and pretty and we really seemed to get on. I didn't have too much loot at the time but her father was quite well off in a middle-class sort of way, so when the question of marriage eventually cropped up after we had been going around with each other for a while, there didn't seem any real obstacle to the idea. We got married in a Kensington registry office and that seemed that. The truth was, though, that I wasn't really ready for marriage and Claire and I were never truly compatible. In the end a wall was to erect itself between us. I found I couldn't get through that wall to her and, of course, I have my own particular wall which many people have difficulty getting through. I'm really a very private person – so private, indeed, that I'm often a private person even to myself. There are always a lot of silly thoughts going around in my head and then there's this barrier and, underneath that, thoughts I would really like to get at. But I cannot get through there – and I cannot find out why. Living with me is not an easy thing and throughout our marriage, relations between Claire and me were stormy. In addition, I was just beginning to discover that many women could find me attractive and I think I began to resent my loss of freedom.

Professionally, I was still driving myself on to become a really mature and confident musician. I can recognize now that while I played with the London orchestras I felt immature and lacked confidence. I never stopped practising and people used to approach me and ask in some astonishment why I practised so much. 'You play so well,' I was told. Nobody, fortunately, seemed to understand that although I sounded very sure of myself, underneath I lacked confidence. I was after a mastery of the flute similar to the mastery of his weapon shown by a great Zen archer or swordsman. I was seeking a perfection which I alone was capable of comprehending. For example, when I was with Sadler's Wells, I knew the operatic repertoire backwards and could have played *Faust* in my sleep; it was coming out of my ears. But I still lacked experience and knowledge of the orchestral repertoire.

Although I enjoyed much of my work at Sadler's Wells, I found the restrictions on outside work increasingly galling. There were little jobs with the BBC available, there were gigs for small music clubs. But the management kept a tight rein. Two or three times I had to cancel broadcast engagements merely because my presence was demanded at rehearsal of some opera I already knew inside out. A break had to come.

It occurred when the City of Birmingham Symphony staged a major international competition with a first prize of £1,500, £750 for second and £350 for third, as well as other minor awards. This was a substantial amount of money in those days. I applied for leave which the management grudgingly allowed me. Not entirely to my own astonishment, I won first prize in the flute section, thus earning myself £750. To win £1,500 I had to go back and do the second half of the competition, consisting of a straight fight between the winners of all the sections – horn, oboe, clarinet and flute.

I returned to London, saw the management representative at Sadler's Wells, Charles Coverman, who was mainly responsible for keeping us all under control and said, 'Listen, Charlie, I've just won the first bit of this competition which means £750. But I've got to go back and play again next week to win the £1,500 top prize. Will you give me the time off?'

I might as well have asked Charlie Coverman for all the money in his bank. The whole idea was unthinkable; I'd already had time off, and so on. Finally, I said, 'Listen, I'll make a deal with you. Give me the time off and if I win the competition, I'll agree to leave the orchestra and you can get yourself somebody who'll play night and day for you.'

'What happens if you don't win?' demanded Charlie.

I eyed him coldly. 'Then I'll leave anyway. OK?'

In Birmingham, the international jury could not decide between myself, a French oboe-player called Maurice Bourgue and a Roumanian clarinettist. So they split the additional £750 between us.

I spent the money repairing the roof on my house and one or two other things while looking for another job.

The really important thing so far as any professional musician is concerned is to make good music. Any artist feels compelled to make something good, to create something great that will make a large number of people happy. The fact that you get paid for doing it is quite another matter. Even 'The Flight of the Bumblebee' is not something I embark on lightly. I know that this little piece will give enormous pleasure to a great number of people, so I practise and practise beforehand until it eventually sounds exactly right. To get things right has always been more important to me than making money.

I entered the Birmingham competition, however, with my mind split two or three different ways. More and more I resented the restrictions imposed on us by the management. I was spurred on, too, by my ambitions; deep down I had this vision of myself as a soloist and it seemed to me that only by entering competitions, where I could emerge from the anonymity that surrounds all orchestra members, could I succeed. Lastly, but not least at that time, the prospect of earning myself £1,500 at a single swoop really enticed me.

Many sides of my nature were tugging at me. There was the religious and spiritual side; the artistic side; and finally, and somewhat disastrously, there was the materialistic side. I was really into materialism at the time of my marriage. We ate extremely well and always bought the best wine. It was like dining at the Savoy every day – and quite ridiculous. Now I get up in the morning, have porridge for breakfast, then for lunch cabbage cooked in soy sauce and mixed with brown rice and feel really great and wonder how many years I took off my life eating all the stuff I used to eat.

With my son Stephen on the way, finances could not be ignored, however, and I was delighted to land a job as flautist and piccolo with the BBC Symphony Orchestra. The money was somewhat better than at Sadler's Wells. The BBC proved to be a good mid-stream orchestra and I enjoyed the change and found a bunch of very happy characters there. David Butt was the other first flute and Robin Chapman second and we all got on like a house on fire.

One of the first things I played was Beethoven's Ninth Symphony with Sir Malcolm Sargent.

During rehearsals for Beethoven's Ninth with Sir Malcolm,

he handed me a score for the flute which I was astonished to see had a number of notes written in red. I looked up, perplexed, but was told to play them. 'But this isn't Beethoven,' I objected. 'Beethoven never wrote these.'

'No,' said Sir Malcolm quietly, 'I've written those in myself. Now please play them like a good chap, will you, Galway?' Blushing to the gills I did as I was told of course, and that night the performance seemed fantastic. I know a lot of people didn't like Sargent as a conductor; he could be a great source of annoyance to certain orchestras. His manner of telling people how to do things got a few backs up. He had this very upper-crust way of ordering things as though he were talking down which irritated some people. But frankly it never bothered me and I thoroughly enjoyed playing under him. I also played for him during his last Proms. On the last night the main work was *The Planets*, but I recall piping out those famous bars from the 'The Sailor's Hornpipe' on what, regrettably, turned out to be his last 'last night' of the Proms. Shortly afterwards, terminal illness struck him down.

He had a great attitude towards young people, I thought, and certainly was always most courteous and polite to me, even though I must have messed things up at times. He never made any great hassle, however, and just explained what he wanted and that was that. Once, there was a right to-do. I usually had a nap in the afternoon before a concert and I woke up feeling great – for a change – and looked at the bedside clock and read 4.45. So I ambled downstairs, looked at some rubbish on TV that was totally unfamiliar and remarked to Claire, 'I don't think I've ever seen this programme before.'

'That's because you're not usually here at this time,' she said.

'But it's only five o'clock!'

'No, there's been a power cut,' she said. So I rang up the GPO Speaking Clock and discovered it was 7 pm. And I was due to play at the Albert Hall at 7.30! Claire called a taxi while I gathered my dress clothes together. I bundled myself into the taxi, told the cabman to drive like crazy and changed in the cab. Somehow I made it, but was so knocked out by the excitement and rush that, although I was due to play in the first piece, I had to find the toilet first. In the Albert Hall, the toilets, of course, are miles from anywhere. So I charged down, then charged back only to find Sir Malcolm waiting patiently. Another conductor might have bawled me out. But Sir Malcolm just gave me one of his smiles and said, 'Come on, Galway, we can't have this sort of thing here.'

Doing the Proms is really exciting. The atmosphere is really special and I know of nothing like it anywhere else in the world. Nowhere else, certainly, but at the Albert Hall, would one find the audience yelling out something like 'Bravo, Jimmy!' when you play an orchestral piece. I remember the shock that ran through the Berlin Philharmonic when we did a one-night stand there. Lothar Koch played the note for the orchestra and the Prommers sang it and then shouted 'Bravo, Lothar!'. Nothing like that, I assure you, happens in Berlin.

Each night after the performance the entire orchestra adjourned to the 'Ninety-Nine', a pub round the corner. It is so-called because the Royal College has ninety-eight rooms and the pub makes the ninety-ninth.

Sir Malcolm was, I believe, everyone's dream of a great conductor. Personally I not only found him charming but amusing. Once he decided to demonstrate to me on his baton how he wished me to play a certain passage on the flute. I still regret that I did not have a camera with me at the time for the great man played his 'flute' with all the keys on the wrong side. I also remember a story he told once. He had come across this guy in Cairo playing just three notes on the flute. When he passed through the city six months later, the guy was still playing the same three notes. 'Why are you still playing those three notes?' he inquired.

'Because everybody is busy looking for these notes – and I'm the only one who has found them.'

Piccolo-playing I found tedious; there is very little good music for it. All that I can really remember about playing it is the occasion when Pierre Boulez ticked me off, insisting that my E flat was out of tune. In fact, the guy who had played in E flat just before me *had* been out of tune but Boulez hadn't noticed it. So I was forced to play it as the idiot before me had done – out of tune. The degree of concentration necessary was minimal. I often found myself thinking of gas and electricity bills or girls instead of following the music.

The dream of every musician in Britain is to play with the LSO which undoubtedly deserves its reputation as one of the foremost orchestras in the world. I had been pestering them for some time to give me an audition but they refused, insisting that I was not sufficiently well acquainted with the repertoire.

I finally convinced them I was worth hearing, and went along one day to the Kingsway Hall to play a concerto and some of the orchestral repertoire. To my astonishment, there was no piano. 'Even Sadler's Wells can afford a piano!' I protested. There was nothing for it, however, but to play unaccompanied, which I did, and I was not at all surprised when they delivered the classic phrase, 'Don't ring us, we'll ring you.'

I had already joined the BBC Symphony when the LSO actually *did* ring. Would I do a gig – a concert at the Guildhall? It turned out to be a performance of Mozart and Haydn – the Haydn piece was *The London Symphony* which the composer wrote when he visited London. The LSO was a superb orchestra in those days, very fine, and I was astonished how easy it was to play with it. Just before the interval and during Barry Tuckwell's horn concerto, I had a free period. With George, a Scot who played the trumpet and was very fond of malt whisky, I repaired to the nearest pub to refresh myself with a glass of lemonade. When we were walking back to the Guildhall together, this rather dignified personage stopped us.

'I', he boomed, 'am Ernest Fleischmann!' He made it sound as though God were talking. Believe it or not, I had no idea who Ernest Fleischmann was. 'Who did you say you were?' I asked.

'Ernest Fleischmann,' he repeated.

'All right,' I said, 'I mean *who* are you? What do you want?'

Beside me, my Scottish friend was doing his nut. *He* knew who Ernest Fleischmann was, all right. He began cackling like an old hen in his appreciation of the situation.

'Would you mind, sir,' expostulated Fleischmann indignantly. 'I would like a word with this gentleman alone. Please leave us.' To his credit, malt whisky and all, George cleared off.

'I am the General Manager of the LSO,' explained Fleischmann, 'and we'd like to offer you the job of first flute with the orchestra, Galway.'

Proverbial feathers for the knocking over with were then certainly the order of the day. I was absolutely staggered that after all my attempts merely to obtain an audition I should be hired in this way. Worse, that only a few weeks after I had quit Sadler's Wells and signed up with the BBC as a piccolo-player, I should be offered the job of first flute with the LSO. When I had recovered from the shock and had time to sort things out, I explained about the BBC.

'We'll see what can be done,' Fleischmann assured me. He was as good as his word and the BBC finally agreed to release me.

Suddenly, therefore, I found myself in the big time. My salary, to begin with, more than doubled – to £100 a week. Not that the money meant all that much to me compared with feelings of prestige and satisfaction. World-famous names buzzed about my head and I realized that many legendary figures were now actually my colleagues.

The demands, of course, were terrific and if I imagined I had worked hard before, I now learned something of what hard work was really like. Basically I knew only the operatic repertoire. So I had to learn what amounted to a whole new language. For a time, I lead a perilous existence, scraping through continually by the skin of my teeth. Practice and preparation became sheer murder. It particularly involved listening to records. Once Colin guest-conducted us and on the way home asked me, 'Jimmy, how do you manage in the orchestra with all this new stuff?'

'I listen to records,' I replied.

Colin is one of the world's most honest men. 'Yes, I do that myself. It's a very quick way of learning things.'

Listening to records is, in fact, of enormous help. With a new repertoire you not only have to learn a new language so to speak, but to teach yourself a feel for it. Nor is there any point in simply learning your individual part – say a few notes of 'The Blue Danube'. You have to discover how the whole piece goes to make your contribution count. Records, therefore, are a shorthand method of enabling you to appreciate the whole.

If it was terrific, musically, to play with the LSO, it was also, politically speaking, a disastrous experience. It soon became clear that everybody connected with the orchestra was hypersensitive. I wasn't used to people *not* talking to each other. In Sadler's Wells, for instance, everybody was very relaxed. If you thought the fellow next to you needed to play a note louder or sharper you had no hesitation in asking him. And he never took offence. There was freedom of speech with everybody respecting everybody else and the aim was that the full orchestra should achieve the best results, not the individual alone. With the LSO, however, you had to keep tight rein on your tongue. If you asked someone to play a note louder, you were treated like a spy of the management or a tell-tale who was trying to get that person a bad name so that he could be fired. Then there were the cliques of very good players who were up against the cliques of merely good players. The whole thing became dreadfully involved in this way and really upset me. It had always seemed to me that there are very good musicians and pretty indifferent musicians but that those who are good have to help the less talented so that all can pull together for the good of the orchestra. In the end there was a bust-up between Fleischmann, Barry Tuckwell, the chairman of the orchestra, and Istvan Kertesz, the principal conductor, and I felt I couldn't stand it anymore so, shortly after André Previn was appointed principal conductor, I left. I had thought everything would be peaceful and quiet but this was the beginning of my dream being shattered because it never is.

This was a pity because there were some magnificent players with the orchestra. John Georgiadis was leader, Nelson Cook, first cello, Gervase de Peyer, clarinet, Roger Birnstingl, who now plays in Switzerland, bassoon, and Barry Tuckwell, first horn. There were associations with the great guest stars – Zubin Mehta, who conducted the LSO's first performance of

The Rite of Spring, Gennadi Rozhdestvensky, Rostropovich and others.

Among the great things also to come out of my association with the LSO were the overseas tours. One of the best I had was with Rostropovich in the US where I had the privilege of meeting Marcel Moyse for the first time. The concerts were staged at Carnegie Hall and I shared the job of principal flute with my old friend William Bennett. To be frank, this was something I had not wanted, but the LSO at that time was seeking to establish itself along the lines of the Berlin Philharmonic and other continental orchestras of stature and was having difficulties owing to a lack of money. I objected vigorously to having a co-principal thrust upon me, but after an argument with the board of directors I surrendered and suggested that if they insisted on hiring a co-principal then they had better sign William Bennett 'because he's the best'.

In the event neither William nor I were any too happy with the arrangement. For the first and only time in our lives, our friendship could not hide the fact that neither of us was any longer prepared to play second fiddle to the other. In Berlin I did not object to sharing the job of principal flute because when I played then the other principal had time off; if he played, I didn't have to turn up. But William and I *both* had to play with the LSO in the same concert with, perhaps, me playing the first half of a concert and William the second. I resisted this all the way, my attitude being that I was *the* solo player and would brook no rival. It was this kind of ham-fisted method of doing things that eventually helped to drive me from the LSO.

Shortly before we left for America I learned that Marcel Moyse was still alive and living not far from New York. One day, with Richard Taylor, the second flute, I flew up to Vermont to see Moyse. The village of Battleboro turned out to be a picturesque New English setting and we walked up a hill and found a legend branded into a wooden door saying 'Marcel Moyse. Please come in.'

We entered and found the great man and his wife both fast asleep in front of an enormous TV set which was then showing a Western – with the sound turned up *fortissimo*.

Moyse was then about seventy-six and looked so incredibly old that I was almost afraid to waken him. Anyhow I shook him gently and he opened his eyes and said, 'Where you have been?' He had been living in the States for twenty-odd years but his English remained still rather strange.

I explained why we were there so he said, 'Come back in morning and play.' This we did and I had my first close-up encounter with the great master. I didn't quite know what to play for him, but in the end played a Bach sonata, that B Minor Sonata that I had been afraid to play with John Francis because then I could not understand it. In among all these notes that Bach had written Moyse showed me where the melody was and how when the same tune comes again, but in a different key, it means something different. It was a real awakening. It was at this point, in fact, that I realized there was a sort of sunshine in flute-playing which I lacked and which he was now demonstrating to me. It was the *way* he told me that impressed me. It was his enthusiasm which burned right into me and came out again from my flute.

Next day I went along again and this time I played Schubert. He explained in terms of the voice how to play the flute, that was, to relate it to singing. To quote from a singing manual by Giano Nava:

> The mechanical part of the art of singing or flute-playing is almost entirely acquired by the exercise of vocalization which consists in singing a given *solfeggio* using merely the vowels. That is to say, on the flute you do not use harsh attack but you play softly and beautifully. This is the only way of developing the tone, of rendering it flexible and ready for all the material difficulties of flute-playing. The execution of this type of exercise must be preceded by some preparatory exercises in order to acquire the art of strengthening and softening the tone at pleasure, of emitting the voice or the tone full and broad, of well-regulating the respiration, of passing from one register to another imperceptibly, of carrying the tone, of connecting the sounds, swelling them and diminishing them by imperceptible degrees, of detaching them. And lastly the art of executing all the ornaments of singing with grace, lightness and precision.

What he was getting at was that there should be another dimension in the flute which should consist of colours and nuances which did not then exist in my playing. Moyse had written some exercises on the principles of vocalization and he demonstrated in his little room how I should do them. It was a simple little room, wooden-walled, hung with photographs of his wife and son and friends. His kitchen was a rambling affair with a billiard table – he played snooker – and the whole house was a very simple shack. To me, however, the experience I gained on that hill was worth everything I possessed because when I came down again my whole attitude to playing had been changed. These lessons from Moyse turned out to be the first major breakthrough in the way of musical expression on my part. He was the first to put it all into words and to make me seek to relate my music to nature, something which I want to underline.

Zubin Mehta seemed to me to be one of the greatest conductors to take the LSO. After *The Rite of Spring*, we rehearsed Strauss's '*Heldenleben*' where there is a tricky part for the flute. It is the first picture Strauss gives of the enemy and the flute has to be played very staccato, very hard. I called out, 'Zubin, can you make your beat a bit larger there, make your gestures a bit bigger, because I can't really see them?'

'My dear Jimmy,' called out Zubin, 'I've often had requests from *deaf* flute players – but this is the first time I've had one from a *blind* one.'

It was Zubin's first performance with a major British orchestra and I really admired him. Another fine conductor was Claudio Abbado who did Tchaikovsky with us. At one point in the programme we came across a passage which suddenly became so quick that I realized I couldn't play it. This is a nightmare situation. Fortunately for me the music was particularly loud at this point and I said to Richard Taylor, my second, 'Dick, I hadn't expected this so quick – I can't play it.' In a flash, Richard replied, 'Jimmy, leave all the *tuttis* to me, that's what I'm here for and you play all the solos, that's what you're here for.' It was one of the nicest gestures a musician could hope for from a colleague and I could not have appreciated it more.

Two other great conductors with whom I played were Leonard Bernstein and Gennadi Rozhdestvensky. I did a series of Tchaikovsky with the latter at the Albert Hall. He is a really marvellous figure, a really expressive man with a conducting range extending from the very deep to the highly frivolous. For example, he once put his baton under his left armpit and gazed at someone over the top of his glasses while the orchestra played on – I believe he often does this. On another occasion, during the last movement of Tchaikovsky's Sixth Symphony, the *Pathétique*, he fixed his eyes on the gong-player as though trying to hypnotize him. There is one gong note only in this movement and when I glanced across I nearly cracked up – the gong player was fast asleep. Gennadi, I think, was trying to hypnotize him *awake*.

Rozhdestvensky conducted some of the LSO concerts in America when Kertesz fell ill and also conducted the Berlin Phil while I was with it. He loved to play really spectacular music such as Bartok's *The Miraculous Mandarin.* Once, after a stunning performance of *Daphnis and Chloë*, a real knock-out, he came right into the orchestra and dragged me out to take a special bow. Musicians are human beings, contrary to a belief held in certain quarters, and it is gestures such as these that really make individual instrumentalists play their heads off. In the last analysis, it is the secret of great conducting. When I was with the Royal Philharmonic, for instance, I was never aroused to such heights by Rudolf Kempe who, technically was among the finest. He never acknowledged whether I was good or bad. Perhaps he sensed that I thought his conducting a bit dry. I like romantic conductors, guys who make the music get to the hearts of the people, and not all these fellows who look at you with piercing eyes like a traffic cop. Music is to do with the heart – not where the cars and buses are going. Eugene Ormandy and André Previn also gave me great pleasure. During the flute movement of the last movement of Mahler's Tenth, I saw tears streaming down Eugine Ormandy's face, I also played with Previn when he did the Rachmaninov Second Symphony for the first time, music he made famous. Kertesz, of course, was a superb conductor and I played with the orchestra for all the recordings of the Dvořák symphonies.

There were some really fine musicians and good friends with the LSO and it was a very hard-working, hard-drinking orchestra – which I believe it still is. But this division of sides within the group troubled me. If you were drinking with one bunch – and we all used to enjoy a pint in Kingsway after a performance – then the other bunch tried to tag you as a member of that gang. All I wanted to do was to be friendly with everybody and to extract some fun out of life with jokes and a bit of drinking when we weren't working. When it reached a certain pitch, I got fed up and decided to move.

I still recall Kertesz (who had already made up his own mind to move) trying to coax me to stay. Isaac Stern was in Kertesz's office at the time and he joined in the effort, but my mind was made up. When I think of it it is extraordinary how orchestras hate you to move. For instance, when I told the RPO I was going to Berlin, the chairman of the orchestra Elgar Howarth gave me this long spiel about why I shouldn't go to Berlin, knocking both Karajan and the Berlin Phil enough to scare the pants off me. And then again, when I announced I wanted to leave Berlin, there was Herbie sending the first oboe to me with instructions to 'get Jimmy to change his mind'. It is both funny *and* serious in its own sort of way, for these guys never really appreciate what kind of stew is in the pot. Oddly enough the only orchestra that never tried to coax me to stay was Sadler's Wells – that is, after I ceased to be a learner and became a full professional – but I think that Colin Davis and I were such good friends that he could read my mind and understood my reasons as well as I did myself.

In my private life at this time, I was not *too* unhappy; not that I was happy either. My son Stephen was about two now. There were a lot of hassles between Claire and me because she complained – rightly perhaps – that a wife was entitled to see more of her husband than she was seeing of me. The fact was that I was practising hard and playing hard with the LSO and that I did like to spend a little time in the pubs afterwards – but Irishmen, anyway, are notoriously bad husbands in certain respects, tending to live life in a more Victorian manner, perhaps. The partnership idea is not quite so developed in Ireland yet as in America and Britain. I don't think Claire relished me rehearsing at three o'clock in the morning either. Particularly if the neighbours complained. When people complained of my playing at night, I always desisted. If they got uptight during the day, I'm afraid I just kept going. But I used to practise and teach a lot when with the LSO and had started doing little bits of solo work at this time, although eventually I found the all-modern music we specialized in much too boring.

I never found Stravinsky either difficult or boring because if you listen carefully there are quite a number of marvellous tunes in his work. I think it is only when one is asked to play some of the younger composers, such as Boulez, Stockhausen and Messiaen that life becomes a bit taxing. I might be a bit behind the times here, but so far as I'm concerned I cannot sing a single tune that either Boulez or Stockhausen ever wrote because I don't understand their music. To me, music is melody and melody music. But this question of *enjoying* music is a highly personal thing. For instance, when I was a kid and played second flute in Belfast with Havelock Nelson's Studio Strings orchestra (made up mainly of doctors and schoolteachers and people like that) we played Schubert's Third Symphony, many years later I recorded the same symphony with the Berlin Philharmonic under Karl Boehm. It sounds nonsense – but to this day I still prefer the Irish version.

I am not anxious to nag on about the LSO, but the sort of trade-union mentality they exhibited during my days there also helped to turn me off. Once, during a rehearsal of Sibelius's Fifth Symphony, they actually walked out on Leonard Bernstein. Bernstein was used to taking command of an orchestra and making it play the music *his* way. Things weren't going too well, so he stopped to give us some of his ideas. Then he began to conduct again, having explained that he was not just prepared to stand there and beat two in a bar and take what came along. On the dot of 9.30, the LSO simply downed tools and strolled off. I cannot think of any other great orchestra in the world who would treat a major musician and great conductor like Bernstein in this way. For Bernstein the contrast with New York must have been staggering. Certainly, it completely amazed me!

My contract with the Royal Philharmonic was very satisfactory; a guaranteed minimum of £4,000 a year, which was reasonable bread in those days. The difference in quality, however, was perceptible. The LSO was on the crest of a wave then, the RPO in a bit of a trough between two big crests. It is not star players who make an orchestra, but the small people of whom little is ever heard. For example, the second violin of the Berlin Phil would be capable of leading any London orchestra – including the LSO. When there was a vacancy for second violin in Berlin, we had kids from all over Europe, who had won major competitions, turning up to audition. Money is part of it all. Back in the late 1960s when I joined Karajan, I was in for £12,000 a year, which put Berlin only second to the New York Metropolitan Opera orchestra; today, with the appreciation of the Deutschmark and the fall of the US dollar, Berlin is probably ahead. With the big money comes quality and with prestige and quality comes success. When I was with the LSO, it had already got itself into this business of star names, TV performances and recordings – those areas where the loot is made – which was why the LSO, technically, was better than the RPO at the time. The rank-and-file were better because they were better paid and so rank-and-file jobs attracted better musicians.

I took part in one tremendous American tour with the RPO when we criss-crossed that enormous country in a Greyhound bus. We played Stravinsky's *Firebird* and Brahms's Fourth Symphony at Carnegie Hall under Vaclav Neumann, now chief conductor of the Czech Philharmonic. It was a most agreeable tour, with visits to many nice places and quite a few good parties, but the problem of 'wet' and 'dry' states created problems for us thirsty itinerants. Before we entered a 'dry' state, the bus driver would have to pull up at a supermarket so that we could load up with a couple of hundred cans of beer; what we needed, of course, were beer-drinking camels. The journeys were deadly boring and we did nothing but play cards all day – which was all right for me because I'm lucky at cards and I made quite a bit of change. But the tediousness needled some fellows. Elgar Howarth was driven to such an extreme that he actually composed a trumpet concerto during the journeys – a fantastic feat of concentration.

Tours are full of hidden perils, of course. I had already developed a slight toothache before going to the US and my dentist had put something on it to calm it down until I got back. We were near the Mexican border when this tooth really began to act up. Next thing Adrian Brett was knocking at the door with the local flute-player. 'You got toothache?' inquired the LFP.

'Yaaaargh!' I said.

'OK, I fix you with my own dentist.'

Well, we saw the dentist who said I had an abscess and the whole thing needed special treatment. I knew that hospitals and doctors cost small fortunes in America, so I was busy weighing up the merits of abscesses versus greenbacks when the dentist said his old professor was a genius at this sort of thing and they would take me to La Jollia (a name which I thought entirely inappropriate) to see the prof. The prof said the Mexican equivalent of 'dear, dear, good gracious' and intimated that I needed an operation. By this time I was really weeping for the National Health Service. Suddenly he said, 'You insured, gringo?'

'Yaaaargh, maybe,' I made further incredible noises, the gist of which was that I thought the orchestra had insured us.

'OK' he said brightly. 'I operate. You insured, OK, your orchestra pay. You not insured – have it on the house!'

That night, after the abscess had been drained, I went to bed with *fifteen* pillows propped up under me, for I had been warned not to lie down. My old chum Derek Wickens, who had brought me into the RPO in the first place, was sleeping in the bed next to me (we all doubled up during the tour). At 3 am I woke to find Derek putting me back into bed again. Apparently I kept wandering about. So on top of everything else, I had become a sleepwalking nutcase.

Practical jokes are part of the risks during tours – but practical jokes have a habit of misfiring. In those days I was heavily dependent upon glasses (I don't need them anymore) and when one day they vanished I thought the end of the world had come. I was still a pretty insecure guy in those days and my various complexes and assorted feelings were rarely helped when I saw conductors taking a succession of bows, while I never even got a pat on the back from the door-keeper. Many conductors often ignore the *feelings* of the instrumentalists who can get to feel a bit downtrodden at times. Once, after I had played '*L'Aprés Midi*' for Karajan at Salzburg, he sent for me and said, 'Jimmy, you really played terrific tonight, really marvellous.' This was the kind of gesture that makes Karajan the greatest. But during this tour I had talked myself into feeling not appreciated. So I had got into drinking and smoking and staying up late every night and in general cursing the lot of an orchestral musician. It really was murder, being cooped up in a bus for six hours every day, then experiencing the strain and intense concentration involved in major concerts. When my glasses vanished, I felt near the end of my tether. Only when the son-of-a-gun who had taken them realized that his 'joke' was no joke but could easily wreck the orchestra's performance, did they mysteriously turn up again. The mental stress I had been subjected to, however, was considerable.

There were laughs, of course. During a concert of Schubert's Unfinished Symphony, given at Red Rocks, Colorado, Roy Jowett somehow managed to get water in his clarinet and when he blew it it sounded so funny that the whole orchestra joined in with the ten-thousand-strong audience in such gales of laughter that the second clarinettist was unable to take over. And the places we played – once it was in a hall normally used for dog shows, then, on another occasion a rodeo ground. As for American food! – we were stacked up over Chicago in a plane when the stewardess announced that she was serving 'bread sandwiches'. I've eaten some queer sorts of sandwiches in my time – everything except goat, I think – but this sounded one for the book. Yet there it was – two slices of white bread on the outside and a slice of brown in the middle.

Back in London, life resumed its uneasy tempo. I desperately wanted out of my orchestral seat – if only on a temporary basis – and the RPO manager, Raymond Few, promised me four flute concertos a year, which would have kept me happy. Unfortunately they never materialized and that made me feel even more fed up. When managements get you into a slot, they do really like to keep you there – which, I suppose, is only human nature. But having been promised the concertos, not getting them seemed pretty hard to me. Meanwhile, my private life, if far from being a mess, didn't seem idyllic, either. Claire and I were into a really deep argument at the time – what we would call 'a barney' in Ireland. This also helped to depress me a bit.

Derek Wickens, John Constable, the pianist, and I then got together to do some concerts of chamber music. I also did a fair amount of 'session' work – that is backing some of the pop groups (no, I never played backing for the Beatles). I also did other commercial work – recordings for films, that sort of thing. One score I really enjoyed doing was Richard Rodney Bennett's music for *Far From The Madding Crowd*. It is particularly satisfying that now Richard has written a new flute concerto for me.

Frankly, I don't think I'm an envious or jealous person in any real sense of those words. Competitive, yes; prepared to fight my corner, yes. The others, no. Yet I continued to feel niggled by the lack of appreciation and recognition that is the fate of an orchestral instrumentalist. It is soul-destroying work in so many different ways and literally does drive one to drink – at least it drove me to drink (if only a pint or two at a time). Often when I thought I had played rather well and some of the orchestra thought so too, it niggled me that there would be no mention in the press next day. This *lack* of attention might not have been quite so bad if it hadn't been for the fuss made of conductors who, if the truth were told, had often had to be dragged through the music by the orchestra – or by a section of it. I remember one conductor getting rave reviews for a performance of a Mahler symphony which in truth had been an appalling performance. Geza Anda, the pianist, could not believe what this particular conductor did to his concerto either.

Spiritual development, so far as I was concerned in those days, came much more from the bottle than from the other source. Intellectually, I found myself at a standstill. I read the odd book,. but nothing sparked me off. I seemed to be spiritually dead. I was always OK for a laugh, but inside myself I felt terribly sad. I tried to give the impression of being happy because I don't think it right to ooze depression all over your fellow men but inside I was disturbed, vaguely troubled, sad.

It would be nice to say that I felt I had begun to rise above my background by this time, but the truth is that my humble origins still haunted me. Once at a party in Washington I was chatting with the boss of a big Chicago bank and although I was standing there talking to him, I really wasn't there at all. I was still afraid. Inside me I was wondering what this guy was thinking of me, how he regarded me. I tried to tell myself that this was all insecure rubbish but it still wasn't easy to get rid of the feeling. Imperceptibly things did improve, but to this day, for better or for worse, I am still the same kid from Carnalea Street that I always was. That is, I still feel it. Even when I read a newspaper headline or article acclaiming me 'the greatest flautist of his generation', deep down I know I'm still wee Jimmy Galway from Carnalea Street.

CHAPTER TWELVE

I decided to leave the Royal Philharmonic Orchestra and go to Berlin because the idea of playing with the world's greatest orchestra and the man who, indisputably, must be regarded as the emperor of all conductors – and I do not overlook the claims of Solti, Bernstein and others – attracted me immeasurably. I badly needed something to lift me from my slough of despond. Herbert von Karajan and the Berlin Philharmonic beckoned to me like a lodestar.

To be beckoned is one thing; to get beckoned is another. I had first heard of von Karajan and the Berlin Phil – in the sense of possibly being connected with them – while I was travelling back from Sheffield by car with a friend of mine. We had both been playing a gig with the RPO and had spent four hours rehearsing for a two-hour concert of new music, all of which had left me feeling very depressed indeed. The whole performance, the whole concept of one-night stands of this nature, had so got on my nerves that I began grizzling fiercely, slashing away at the whole system. 'Look, Jimmy, why don't you try for the Berlin Phil?' my friend interrupted. 'The Berlin Phil?' my mind went cold. 'But that's in

Germany.' I was quite taken aback at the idea.

'Yes,' he said.

The idea of a *British* flute-player attempting to get a job in Germany's *première* orchestra, stunned me. The facts were, however, that the Berlin Phil, particularly under Karajan, had begun to cast its net ever more widely. Germany might still produce great musicians, but might not there be an instrumentalist in Lapland who was better than any German? The world was Karajan's oyster. Suddenly the question was: could little Jimmy Galway get in there and be a pearl in that oyster?

At this time my marriage, too, was getting into an increasingly strange groove. Every day I was going further and further away from my wife. I was coming to realise that I had either married too soon or was not cut out for marriage or, possibly, had married the wrong girl entirely.

A few days later at the Rising Sun pub in Islington, a friend of mine called Martin Nicholls offered to obtain for me details of an advertisement which he had seen in a German magazine. His wife was German and she had read the advertisement which invited musicians to apply for an audition with the Berlin Phil. Armed with this, I went to see another friend called Stanislav Heller, now professor of harpsichord in Freiburg, who helped me write a letter in German. We really pulled out all the stops on this but, incredibly, I had to wait for another eighteen months before I received an invitation to audition. By this time, of course, I had pretty well given up hope.

On 29 January 1969, I flew directly to Munich where, according to a letter I had received, I was to appear at 12 o'clock midday in the Deutsches Museum (the orchestra was on tour at the time). I found myself in an emotional, even nervous, state that day, really edgy. That morning, Heathrow had been snowbound and the flight had been delayed. And then, as we flew into Munich and I saw all the snow piled up, I remembered the crash of the Manchester United football club at this airport – which did nothing to lift my spirits either. Anyway I got into a taxi, gave directions to the driver and was eventually deposited in front of the museum. I found people milling about everywhere with nobody prepared to listen to me. Eventually I ran to earth Dr Wolfgang Stresemann, the orchestra's intendant and the son of the German foreign minister at the time of the Weimar Republic which preceded the Hitler regime. 'But Mr Galway', protested Dr Stresemann, 'the audition has already taken place!'

I stared at him in astonishment. I had heard of German efficiency but this really was the limit. OK, so it was now 12.05 – but surely five minutes wasn't that important. 'But it's only five past twelve!' I exclaimed. 'No, no!' He almost brushed me aside, hands gesticulating. '*Nine* o'clock. We sent you a telegram. Nine o'clock!'

'I never received any telegram. The letter says *twelve*.'

This information didn't appear to impress him at all. According to him, there had been a fantastic audition. Flautists from half of Europe. And they had already decided on somebody.

'I've come all the way from London,' I pointed out.

'We will pay your fare,' he replied.

'It's not that!' I retorted angrily. 'Having come all this way, at least I'd expect you to have the good manners to listen to me play the flute. How do you know I'm not better than any of the others?'

My Irish logic really did appear to impress him, or perhaps it was the suggestion that Germans lacked good manners. Anyway it was my first introduction to this particular sort of German hardness. *You should have been here at nine, why weren't you and that's that!* None of this rather easy-going manner you get in Ireland or the half easy-going manner you get in England. So I had felt I had to be rude back.

'Wait here, please,' said Stresemann stiffly and disappeared out of the door. While he was away, I took out my flute and just gave it a toot to make sure it was still working. Then I heard the orchestra rehearsing nearby so I ambled out and looked into the rehearsal room and saw a few flute players I knew, then ambled out again.

A little later Stresemann reappeared. 'Galway!' he said quite sharply, 'Come and play. The Maestro will hear you.' I had never heard anybody called Maestro before and thought it had something to do with cooks at the Savoy or Dorchester or somewhere. Anyhow I followed him out and into another room amd mounted the platform where I marched up to the pianist who was seated there and handed him my music. Below me in the stalls sat the whole orchestra.

The pianist looked at the Ibert Flute Concerto I had handed him which I had played the day before at a BBC concert in Cardiff.

'This isn't a piano audition,' he pointed out. 'You must play Mozart.'

Well, I hadn't rehearsed any Mozart but I said OK and asked him for a couple of bars. I found the piano pitch very high – the pitch in Germany is always higher than in England – but I rapidly adjusted to it and began on the Mozart flute concerto. I had just got to the end of the first page when a voice from the audience shouted out, 'Right! Now play a cadenza!' I didn't know who had shouted but the voice sounded authoritative (in fact, it was Karajan himself). I didn't quite know what to play, but when I turned the page there was a cadenza which I had learned in Belfast while I was still being taught by Muriel Dawn. Like a man coming home, I swung into it with tremendous *élan* and simply steamed through it.

'Right, fine. Now play *Daphnis and Chloë*,' came this voice from the stalls. So I played that – which, fortunately, I knew from memory. Then, '*Play L'Après Midi*'. I did that. 'Right, now play "Heldenleben".' So I did that and then Brahms's Fourth. Karajan kept shouting at me all the most difficult bits of the flute repertoire and it occurred to me that this was an extraordinary bunch because they had not given me any music to play from. They were forcing me to play everything from memory. Then Karajan said, 'Wait outside.'

All this 'do this' or 'do that' without a 'please' or a 'thank you' had begun to needle me a bit. I really was beginning to stir up a real antagonism towards this bunch. Outside I was joined by those members of the orchestra who were not allowed a vote (a player is not allowed a vote during his first year's 'trial period'). Then Stresemann turned up again. 'We want you to play again,' he announced. 'Fine,' I said and followed him into the concert hall.

This time I found four other guys there – two were from Germany, one from Denmark and the other from France. We were told to stand in line and Karajan shouted, 'Now, from left to right, play *A Midsummer Night's Dream*.' This time the music, was supplied and each of us played in turn. 'Now Brahms's Fourth,' demanded Karajan which he followed with '*Heldenleben*'. Starting from the left, all five of us played these pieces in turn. Then von Karajan made us play from right to left. 'Wait outside!' came the peremptory voice finally. 'Thank you very much.'

So we all shambled out and stood around like a bunch of sheep. We weren't kept waiting long. In a few minutes, Dr Stresemann reappeared. He marched right up to me, grabbed me by the hand and shook it. 'Mr Galway,' he said grandly, 'congratulations! You are now the principal flautist with the Berlin Philharmonic. When can you start?'

'Listen here,' I said rudely. 'I don't know that I can start at all. I mean, I'm not sure that I *want* to start. Everybody's so rude here. You're all so rude that I don't feel I want to start.'

This was a genuine reaction. But I was also buoyed up by the fact that one of the orchestra members who had been sucking an orange for lunch had come over to me and whispered, 'You know, you're the best, absolutely the best. If they don't give you the job, they're mad.'

Anyhow Stresemann seemed to be quite taken aback by my reaction. He stuttered something about the law in Germany being that if you won an audition, you *had* to take the job. I've no idea whether this is true or not, but putting on my very best Irish accent I said, 'That may be all right for Germans. But who's German around here – I'm not?'

'You cannot leave it like this!' he insisted.

'I'm sorry,' I said. 'I haven't time to stand around here arguing (I knew I would miss my plane if I did not leave soon.) All I can say is that I'll think about it. I am not impressed with the people around here and the way they treat people.'

'Really, I assure you. . .'

'I've got to go home now. But I'll think it over and then write to you and let you know if I'll take the job.' With that I said goodbye and walked out to go back to the airport.

That same evening I was back in London. 'Oh, it's marvellous news,' pronounced Claire in her very mild way. In the Rising Sun, which is a sort of musician's pub, nobody had any doubts either. 'The greatest, Jimmy,' they kept saying, 'the greatest'.

I was left with no choice in the matter, really. So I sat down and wrote saying I was prepared to give the job a trial. I would not put in the full probationary year they expected new members of the orchestra to serve. I would go for a month and if I liked it, then I would stay. In fact, when I returned to Germany, everybody opened doors and wiped chairs for me and so great was the change that I accepted the job – and even agreed to do the probationary period, called the *pro-Bespiel.*

The first piece of music I ever played with the Berlin Philharmonic was Beethoven's Eroica Symphony and it made me realize that I was in a different league altogether. The whole body of strings was superb and the general sound of the orchestra fantastic. At the end I knew I had experienced something really different. I was not quite so taken with the second piece, called 'From The German Soul', by Pfitzner. This seemed to go on for hours and hours. The second flute was Johannes Mertens (who died in 1975) who had come up to me after the audition in Munich and, instead of introducing himself with all this 'Professor this' and 'Herr Doctor' that stuff which they go in for in Germany, had said simply, 'My name is Hans Mertens,' so that we were 'Hans' and 'Jimmy' from the beginning. Before rehearsal Hans said, 'Listen, Jimmy, in this piece there is a big flute solo somewhere, but I don't remember where.' I decided there was nothing much to worry about but took the music home anyway and had a squint through it, but all the stuff looked the same to me (normally you can spot a flute solo a mile off). Anyway, the big laugh came in the first rehearsal. We steamed away until we came to this passage when suddenly I realized that the rest of the orchestra had stopped playing. I gawked down at the score again, but there, sure enough, were notes I had to play. I ploughed on somehow, conscious that this was a *real* solo – not one of those pieces where the instrument you are playing takes the starring part, as it were, but strings keep you company in the background. And what is more, the whole thing was going on . . . . and on . . . . and on. Altogether, I suppose, that piece lasted a good five minutes.

In those days I was often nervous and, faced with a testing piece in what was only my second outing with the orchestra, I really fluffed quite a bit. Wrong note piled on wrong note. I found I could not concentrate and I was also keenly aware that I was playing with an orchestra where every member hopes to outshine the others. Nerves did affect me a lot in those days and I totted up quite a few mistakes in the beginning – which might be good news to any aspiring musicians reading these words. I cannot quite understand why this should have happened because I had no real need to feel anxious. But the hard competitiveness did, regrettably, needle me unduly. The whole Berlin Phil was deep into this competitive thing. For instance Lothar Koch, the oboe-player, always tried to play everything as though it were an oboe concerto. Once in Salzburg, when we played '*L'Après Midi*' and *Daphnis and Chloë* which are big flute pieces, I dropped some of my music on the floor while turning a page. Afterwards, I casually remarked to Koch, 'Hey, did you see that – I nearly dropped all my music that time.' All he said was, 'I am not interested at all.' He meant nothing personal, of course. Basically, all he was interested in was his own performance.

Berlin seemed a strange – and, in many ways, depressing – city to me. I had never seen it in all its heavy pre-war Teutonic grandeur and, towards the end of the sixties, its gimcrack, prefabricated look, interlarded with massive blocks of apartments and houses that had somehow survived or arisen out of the devastation of the Second World War, made it look nothing like as attractive as London or Paris. Indeed, for what it is worth, the central area of my native Belfast appeared to me much more impressive and appealing. Even the behaviour of the people seemed odd to my eyes; men – sometimes women – lashing down beer as thought he world were about to run dry, *at nine o'clock in the morning.* I could not speak German in those days, of course, and wandered around lonely and a bit lost. But I also became aware, perhaps for the first time in my life, of something called 'status'. I discovered that the job of first flute with the Berlin Phil meant something to people outside music. In London if you announce you are first flute with the Royal Philharmonic, it is like declaring you are in charge of the local dustcart – particularly if you are talking to a bank manager. But in Berlin a musician is regarded as a different animal. He is treated with respect, even deference. His problems are taken seriously and people try to assist him. So against the fact that Berlin did not seem too great a place to live in, I had to set a big increase in money; the sheer splendour, excitement and satisfaction of working with the orchestra; a feeling of being personally appreciated. I also knew that it inevitably takes a little time to settle down in a new city, to make new friends, to dig into some form of reasonable social life.

I did not make any immediate or close friends with the other members of the orchestra, most of whom had their own lives to lead and were fairly well settled. Many had long years of service with the orchestra – some as much as twenty-five years. Siegfried Cesliok, the bass trombone player, who had a lovely wife and a beautiful little girl, was helpful. He spoke a little English and showed me around Berlin and helped me look for possible places to live. Then one day Helmut Nicholai came into the dressing-room, introduced himself as 'Nick' and helped me find my first apartment, on Mommsenstrasse where I was soon joined by Claire and little Stephen (nowadays a first-class trumpet-player).

The season with the Berlin Phil was pretty well regularized. It began with a tour which sometimes took in the Edinburgh Festival but inevitably involved the Salzburg Festival and the Lucerne Festival. Karajan is a freeman of the city of Lucerne and he has a special affection for the place, having taken a conducting course there as a young man. After the tour, we normally returned to Berlin and stayed there two months before spending a week in the Federal Republic (West Germany). At Christmas and New Year there were special concerts. Herbie mixed his programmes very cleverly – one year waltzes, the next a Bruckner symphony. At Easter we took off for Salzburg where in my first season. We did '*Götterdämmerung*', the last part of *The Ring*, which was an entirely new sensation for me, as until then I could not stand Wagner. Karajan showed what a quite incredible person he is and I began to understand why he has become a legendary figure in his own lifetime. We spent the first part of the season recording the whole of the opera, with Karajan coaching the singers personally as well as conducting. In Salzburg he not only produced the entire show but conducted entirely from memory. I have talked much of a musician's private life – the domestic squabbles, the hard drinking, the feelings of lack of appreciation, the quest for money and so on. The life of a musician parallels the common lot of mankind; we are not a race apart. Except, that is, when the chips are finally down. In the last analysis we are aware that we are on earth to make and interpret great music and we do find our reward in the expression of our souls' longings. That first night of '*Götterdämmerung*', to put it simply, left me in tears.

After Salzburg, the orchestra generally tours. It might be to Japan or America or anywhere in Europe. Inside Germany we moved about like a procession of royalty. We travelled in our own private train, a blue one, with a placard bearing the legend: 'The Berlin Philharmonic Orchestra under the direction of Herbert von Karajan'. At each little station, the train slowed down so that the local populace could come out to wave to us and pay their respects. We never travelled for longer than four hours a day and at night the train was thoroughly cleaned so that each morning we boarded it feeling fresh and full of pep.

I was the only non-German speaking member of the orchestra and had not yet had time to make good friends. There was not a great deal of socializing between the members of the orchestra, outside of what might be called 'office hours', although these could be pretty elastic as I shall explain. And Claire and I were heading for a bust-up. Our interests were poles apart. She liked talking about politics; I know nothing about them and care less. She never really understood me and my music-making and my crazy Irish ways. She had no feeling for music at all and could not understand why I wanted to sit for hours talking shop to the other musicians with whom I eventually got friendly. In due course, many of them dropped into the flat for a quiet drink and a gossip about our problems, but Claire would never join in and went off to bed instead. She rarely, if ever, came to a concert. I thought, too, that she was materialistic in her outlook. While I was hard up and had little or no savings and we were rubbing along more or less wondering where our next meal was coming from, her attitude did not jar on me particularly. But once I began to get settled in with the orchestra and the monthly cheques arrived to take off some of the pressure, I found her attitude at variance with my own.

Some members of the orchestra did invite us to their homes. Siegfried Ceslick and his wife Helga were very friendly; so, too, was Helmut Nicholai. Christopher Kapler and Peter Geisler also invited us to their homes. But in the end one of my best friends turned out to be somebody who had nothing to do with the orchestra at all. She was Uta Gohring, a painter, who lived in the flat upstairs with her husband Reiner, a doctor of engineering working on metal-fatigue in a local factory.

I first noticed Uta when I saw her walking down Mommsenstrasse one bitter morning. She was approximately eight months twenty-nine days pregnant at the time and fit to bust. In addition, she had the reddest nose I have ever seen on a woman, so intense was the cold. We smiled at each other and I remember feeling sorry for her because the block of apartments in which we lived was like an iceberg. There was a weird central-heating system which involved stoking up the boiler first thing every morning but it did little to help.

Encouraged by the smile, I think, Uta and Reiner invited us up one evening for coffee. We got on so well together that from then on I almost began to live up there. I thought Uta a real scream and enjoyed her company enormously.

My marriage staggered on, going from bad to worse. Perhaps matters were not helped by the fact that I felt imprisoned; locked into a way of life with a person with whom I no longer had much in common. My thoughts and emotions were in turmoil at this time and it was not helped when I bumped into an American woman musician in Venice who talked about being 'free' and 'liberated'. All I really knew, I suppose, was that I wanted out of prison. So one day I simply walked into the flat and announced, 'I think we ought to pack it up, I think I want a divorce.' When Claire, possibly with some justification, brought up material matters, I shouted angrily, 'OK, if you want our house in London, you can have my share. Have it all! I don't really need it and I don't want it and it doesn't mean anything to me.' So I just grabbed hold of a piece of paper and sat down and signed away the property. I shifted out immediately and moved in with Uta and Reiner, sleeping on the floor in a little room they had at the back of their kitchen.

After Claire had left Berlin, the entire house became a kind of commune. The idea of communes had become pretty popular then. Our commune more or less began when I decided there was no point in coming home every day and cooking for myself so I did a deal with Uta whereby I would cook one day for everybody and she would do it the next day. Gradually we extended the idea to a few more customers until eventually we had about fifteen people in the scheme. The whole place became like a restaurant and the idea was great so far as I was concerned, as it meant I had to do the cooking only once every fifteen days or so. One time I made Irish stew for them all and it proved the hit of the season.

They were a great bunch of kids – students, engineers, historians, painters, communists, fascists, anything you like to mention. They were all very nice and helpful, anyway, and worked the schedules round so that they fitted into my engagements with the orchestra. In the end, as is inevitable with these things, there were one or two backsliders and meals did not get served on time and the whole idea collapsed. But while it lasted it seemed a great idea.

With Claire's departure, I entered upon one of the strangest and most emotionally turbulent periods of my life. Single again and in what was basically still a strange city, I began to explore new ideas and new styles of living. During my first year in the city, and while still married to Claire, I had worked hard and diligently to make money, with the intention of setting up a proper house and home and perhaps saving something. But although my income had risen dramatically compared with London standards, I found everything in Berlin incredibly expensive. I had dreamed of being able to afford a Mercedes but it remained a dream.

With Claire's departure, I soon got myself into another sort of world which had nothing to do with money. Much of it had to do with the pop scene and some of it had to do with the super-conservative German society I found myself in. All the kids in the commune were deep into pop at this time and as it isn't really possible to sit around listening to Beethoven all day, I began to listen to the Beatles and other groups along with the rest. I thought the Beatles, in particular, very interesting; they seemed to me very spiritual if you interpreted their music properly. I decided that pop music was not just *bang, bang, bang*, but that if you really listened to all these guys, they were producing tremendous music. I still think the Beatles were important composers. Anyhow, I really got into the Beatles, Pink Floyd and Frank Zappa. Zappa had this crazy-looking beard which I admired so much that I copied it. When Herbie saw me walk into the Philharmonic with my Frank Zappa beard, he almost went up the wall.

He had to keep climbing that wall quite a bit, so far as I was concerned. All sorts of ideas were floating through my head at this time. Although totally apolitical in every sense, I was really against this super-capitalist German society with its starchy, middle-class values. I suppose my own working-class upbringing was busily at work, although I didn't realize it or see it that way. Anyhow, I began to react against dressing up in suits and began wearing very casual clothes. It was so cold in Berlin during the winters that I found I needed a warm coat. I couldn't afford a really elegant fur job so I bought myself this Turkish sheepskin thing which stank to high heaven. The other fellows in the orchestra joked about it: 'You know, Jimmy, only goatherds living up the mountains wear those things.' I know Herbie was also peeved when I bought myself a leather jacket. Nobody wore leather jackets in those days (nowadays you can see Herbie himself wearing one on one of his record sleeves) and when I first walked in, somebody remarked, 'Hey, here's our rocker!' With my Frank Zappa beard, I must have looked a sight. Certainly a lot of comments were made by the others.

Karajan struck back at me in a very effective way. When I first joined the Berlin Phil, most of our work was confined to concerts. But a superb showman – superb entrepreneur, superb producer, superb opera director, superb conductor, superb musician – he had already begun to get things together magnificently and everything was now rolling; concerts, recordings, broadcasts, TV performances, films. Herbie, however, would never allow me to appear in any photograph, film or TV performance – if I played, the cameras had to keep me out of vision. This really annoyed me – it annoyed me that he wanted me to play but not to be seen. I got more and more bolshie therefore – more and more anti-conservative. Today, of course, I realize that Karajan was absolutely right. He is a very careful man, full of excellent judgements. He himself dresses very quietly, if very elegantly, and what it boiled down to was that he didn't want to be seen with an imitation Frank Zappa. I, of course, interpreted him as a square. He was not a square; I had merely got him wrong.

I really had a lot of trouble mentally adjusting to everything around me. I had nobody to talk to properly, just to start with. My lack of fluent German cut me off from a lot of people but I needed something more than just a superficial companionship, anyway. I needed someone with whom I could discuss things deeply, discuss the things that were bugging me. Uta spoke good English but she could not understand what I wanted. She thought she knew what I wanted, but she didn't, because I didn't know myself what I wanted. I couldn't get it together at all.

The effect was strange. There is a book called *The Primal Scream*, about a new kind of mental therapy. They lock you in a hotel room with all the lights on and leave you there for three whole days without sleep or conversation, isolated completely, until you are ready to scream. At the end of the three days, they let you talk to the therapist. Well, I was never as bad as that – but it may give you some idea of the kind of 'prison' in which I found myself.

I fought my way out of that as best I could. Not that I ever allowed my private problems to interfere with my professional life. Despite the hairy coat and leather jacket and the Frank Zappa beard, despite the Beatles records, despite my increasing obsession with eating and drinking and the company of chicks, I turned up every day for my work punctual and ready for anything. Nothing lessened my dedication to Mozart and Beethoven and the whole great canon of classical music. Rehearsals were generally from 10 am to 12.30 and from 4.15 pm to 7.15 p.m. When we were recording, the timings varied slightly. There was some flexibility about which days you worked, but it was not permissible to take a day off without Karajan's permission. Whether you got it or not depended on his mood and also whether the colleague who had to stand in for you was ready to take your place.

As I have mentioned, I was pretty heavily into eating and drinking at this time. My weight now rose until I was fourteen stones – which made me look like a walking Guinness barrel. All the orchestra members were tremendous drinkers, of course. I don't mean that they were a bunch of alcoholics or anything like that, but after a big concert some of us would go out and have a meal and quaff some beer and wine. Whatever my view of Berlin in the architectural sense, I came to appreciate its atmosphere. There were restaurants all over the place and people always out enjoying themselves. So a pattern began to be established: the concert, then a drink in a pub, then a restaurant or perhaps a jazz club, then, when they threw you out of this, someone declaring, 'There's a joint down the road – let's go there,' always ending up at 5 am still celebrating or talking shop. I remember at 5.30 one morning finding myself locked in earnest discussion with a composer about some new flute concerto, when he offered to drive me home. '*Drive*?' I demanded, astonished.

'Yes.'

'You must be out of your mind, Carl.'

'No, no. I can still see – well, just about.'

All this ended with almost dramatic suddenness when I met Annie. A boy friend had taken her to the Philharmonic to hear me play but, as I understand it, she was not too impressed. At this time I had progressed from a Frank Zappa beard to a Solzhenitsyn type and on top of that I wore dark glasses. Put all that on top of the fourteen stones I weighed and there was really no reason why Annie should have been impressed.

A few days later I happened to be in the Akademie der Kunst, home of modern arts in Berlin, listening to a concert of modern music. Sitting just behind me was this girl who sounded about as cracked up about the whole thing as I was. Most of the audience hadn't the slightest idea what was going on, but this was K for *Kultur* and so that was OK with the Germans. Anyway, the audience was taking the whole thing terribly seriously. There was a piece called 'The Sinking of the Titanic' and I got a lot of fun out of this because there was this guy with a violin and he had a circular saw going and he was hitting something else with his bow and ringing bells and heavens knows what else and I thought it ridiculous. So I turned round and said to Annie, 'This is rubbish, isn't it?' and she smiled.

When the performance ended I seized the opportunity to remark to her: 'You shouldn't worry about this sort of rubbish, you know. Come and hear some good flute-playing sometime.'

'Oh,' she said, 'do you know a flute-player called Peter Lukas Graf?'

'Sure, I know him.' I replied. 'Great.'

Peter, it turned out, was a big hero to her. He came from her home town and knew her family well. He had great style, driving fast cars and that sort of thing. Having a mutual friend made everything that much easier.

Well, things progressed pretty fast after that. Annie had a boy friend in Lucerne but was still undecided whether she wanted to marry him or not. She had been unable to make up her mind so her mother had sent her to Berlin to think things over. Anyway, I put her on the train back to Lucerne where she was met by her mother who spotted immediately that there was something in the wind. 'Listen, Annie, are you in love or something?' And so that was that.

We got married in the romantic little church at Platten, just outside Zurich, and set up home in the Mommsenstrasse, though this time in another house from that where I had lived with Claire. It proved to be a terrific flat, so big, indeed, that one Christmas we invited the members of the orchestra around and, as a treat for the neighbours, the Berlin Philharmonic gave a free performance of Beethoven's Eighth Symphony. I came to love that flat. It had two big balconies supported by enormous pillars so that it looked like part of the Reichstag. Although I was earning good money by now, some had to be diverted to Claire and Stephen, while taxes ate into a good deal of the rest, so that it was a while before I could actually boast that I was back in the black. I was happy, however, and enjoying a comfortable standard of living.

I found life with Annie really inspiring because she enjoyed music and the theatre (she took me to see my first German play) and although not a deeply intellectual girl, she was very much into all the sorts of things that interested me. Before marrying me, she had taught eurhythmics, so she had a wide appreciation of many things of which I was only vaguely aware. She had a terrific personality, too, which eased us into many enjoyable social relationships. She looks rather like Lisa Minelli, the film actress. So much so, indeed, that people have approached us in restaurants and asked for her autograph.

In due course Patrick (Paddy) was born. All my children, except Stephen, were born in Berlin – I flew home from America for the birth of my twins, Charlotte and Jennifer. I was present at Patrick's birth. One day I left Annie messing about with the washing machine. When I returned, the kitchen floor was awash. She had forgotten to plug the machine's water outlet into the sink. A little foolishly, if courageously, she had attempted to clean up which was inadvisable having regard to her condition. So I rushed her to hospital and hung around a bit and then decided to stay and see the birth. I thought the whole experience quite phenomenal – like seeing a new island or volcano appear out of an otherwise empty ocean.

CHAPTER THIRTEEN

I think it appropriate here to say something more about Herbert von Karajan and the Berlin Philharmonic Orchestra with both of whom I am proud to have been associated during some of my most formative years. I have no doubt but that the experience, wisdom, knowledge and understanding of music that I gained while playing alongside them has helped considerably to make me the flute-player I am today.

I am constantly asked for my assessment of the Berlin Philharmonic. Any such assessments, of course, cannot be anything but subjective. Yet, despite the technical drive and excellence of some of the great American orchestras, particularly the Chicago Symphony, I believe that over a wide range of music and, in particular, German music, Berlin stands supreme. Even the Berlin version of 'The Blue Danube' has more life, colour, vitality and romance than the rendering by the Vienna Philharmonic. Or so it seems to me.

Today, Karajan must be accorded the plaudits for much of this achievement. The main difference between Berlin and say, the London Symphony, which is still a great orchestra, is that its strength does not lie in the exceptional work of one or two outstanding players. In Berlin, by a process of careful selection and by paying the highest salaries, only the best musicians eventually appear on the Philharmonic platform. The man on the back desk of the second violins is likely to be the equal of the best in Europe. The whole string section of the orchestra is outstanding while the cello and bass sections are unbelievable. In the last analysis, though, it is the way that the whole orchestra had been welded into a team, so that it is no longer a collection of units, some good, some indifferent, that makes it, in my view, the finest orchestra in the world.

Karajan himself has declared, 'I cannot blame anybody else for not getting the results I want. If it's wrong, it's entirely my fault.' Commenting on the Maestro's bravura marathon in New York's Carnegie Hall in November 1976, *Time* magazine wrote: 'In four successive days, he unravelled the musical and spiritual mysteries of Brahms's *A German Requiem*, the Beethoven Ninth Symphony, a double bill of the Mozart *Requiem* and Bruckner's *Te Deum* and the Verdi *Requiem Mass*. Each of these is a work of immense proportions requiring time and money as well as skill to prepare. The average orchestra in the US will usually do one such score a year. As the world of music has known for half a century, there is nothing average about Karajan.'

He was, as I have said, my mentor and father-figure and a great and even noble musician. Nobody else, I believe, can achieve the things he can. His main strength is that he does not conduct like a bandmaster worrying about keeping time, but in such a way that he actually moulds the music into phrases, into shapes, so that it comes out sounding the way he has heard it in his head. He is constantly advising and guiding. I remember standing beside him one day while he was playing the harpsichord in the Brandenburg Concerto and he turned to me and said, 'Jimmy, would you mind just playing it like this.' The request was couched in such a way that I could not possibly have refused it, even if I had thought he was mad. It has all to do with the expression on his face and the light in his eyes. He achieves most of what he wants through charm, for normally he is not a martinet. He has had his share of physical troubles, particularly with a slipped disc, and despite surgery, still experiences pain; as he does not believe in medicines, the suffering is often perceptible. Those of us who knew what he was suffering had come to recognize that if he occasionally seemed crotchety or cranky, there was a reason beyond our own intransigence.

He has, of course, succeeded in 'playing' the orchestra as though playing an organ. He has a tremendous ear for the sound, for the colour of a note, which is a God-given gift. Unquestionably, he learned much from men like Toscanini, but whereas Toscanini was a driver, Karajan has the soul of music in him.

He has a superb feeling and understanding for all the orchestral instruments and is an exceptionally fine pianist himself. That is how he began his career – playing the piano in an opera house. I remember once when he did not like the colour of the violins, he just turned round and demanded, 'Play this chord.' The violins did so. 'Now hold the note long.' Then, 'Right, now, wait a minute – softer.' Then he told them, 'Now just begin the phrase like that. All right?' He would never accept the standard noise.

Yet to give the impression that he organized every phrase, that he made us play every note just as he envisaged it, is to do him an injustice. The first thing Karajan did when the orchestra had finished a piece, was to stand back and allow the audience to applaud them. It is, he was declaring publicly, these men who have achieved this glorious sound, not I. I have merely assisted them not to stray; I have tried to inspire them to their best; I have prevented one section, possibly, from dominating another.

In fact, he allowed us all, as individuals, a great deal of freedom. Often he wanted an effect that I did not approve of. This might have been achieved by means of the traditional way of playing it – but too many traditions have grown up out of the inadequacies of the instrumentalists who laid down the tradition. So I would often play the piece my way because I considered it better instrumentally, as well as musically. If somebody had a good fantasy – and music is merely fantasy – Karajan would give that fantasist all the freedom he needed because he knew that what appeals to an audience is something arising out of the immediate performance, out of something that is happening within the mind of the musician at that moment.

Time had also this to say of the Carnegie Hall performance. 'The Verdi *Requiem* was a marvel of controlled fervour . . . the Brahms *Requiem* seemed cut from velvet rather than the usual broadcloth. Karajan's reading was a subdued rumination, a realisation of the deeply personal utterance the composer drew from the Lutheran Bible . . .'. Having applauded his Mozart and Bruckner, the magazine added, 'Best of all, perhaps, was the Beethoven Ninth'. Summing up, it declared, 'In the currents of sound at Carnegie could be found not only a forceful musical personality but a remarkably complete one; a man's genius, his scholarship, his temper, his power to charm and the wide range of comparative musical judgments he has formed over a lifetime.'

Karajan himself has declared that the orchestra is 'that wall to lean my back on'. His gestures are rarely extravagant and he sometimes conducts with his eyes closed – 'the moulding comes when the orchestra and conductor come together in a sort of union,' he says.

There are those who, because of a kind of envy of Karajan, I suppose, have thought to make snide remarks about his life style. They have made much of his house at St Moritz, the personal aircraft which he pilots himself, the aura of glamour with which he surrounds himself. He cannot walk a street in most of the great cities of Europe without being pursued for his autograph like a pop star.

Yet I found him entirely without 'side', a man above most of the smaller, baser behaviourisms. For instance, in a Germany where most men feel nobodies without a 'Doctor' or 'Professor' as a prefix, he scorns any form of title. He has, of course, endearing little weaknesses; he is crazy about mechanical things and would tinker with a gluepot if you gave him one – and probably end up discovering a petrol-driven motor inside the gluepot driving the glue out.

He remains a very private man. I can never recall him staying on after a concert for a drink with the boys; it was home to bed for Herbie. Nor did he ever invite me to his home; I suspect that with my reputation for unorthodox behaviour he was rather afraid he might wake up the next morning to read headlines in the newspapers: 'First flute bites Karajan's dinner guests'.

He loves driving fast cars very fast indeed. One story they tell of him which I think sums up von Karajan in his private life is about the occasion when he crashed his car driving back to Berlin from Salzburg. He scrambled out of this bent and buckled Mini, walked up to a farmhouse and asked if he could use the telephone. The farmer, of course, did not know him from Adam and was not over-impressed with a guy who could only afford a Mini. In typical Karajan fashion, the Maestro telephoned his chauffeur and a little later, to the farmer's amazement, the man appeared driving Karajan's Rolls-Royce. I always think the story merely proves how modest von K really is. He could so easily, after all, have whistled up his private aircraft.

CHAPTER FOURTEEN

After five years in Berlin, the old restlessness had begun to affect me. Nothing is ever perfect and although, on the whole, I thought the fellows in the Berlin Phil a marvellous bunch, they were also subject to their own ambitions, insecurities and feelings of rivalry. There was a constant psychological warfare being waged that hardly bears thinking about, as this guy or that guy sought to assert himself. There was nothing like the division into warring cliques that had characterized the LSO when I played with them, but everything was not all sweetness and light either. Nor would it be reasonable to expect things to be any other way. It is the nature of human life. And these chaps were musicians, not saints.

I really had nothing to complain about with regard to their behaviour because by now I knew the rules, so to speak, and had adapted accordingly. If one had to be competitive to survive, then I, too, could be competitive. I had clawed my way up from far further down than most of these characters and, in the Darwinian sense, I was a survivor. Nor had I any problems about self-confidence. With due modesty, I knew that the orchestra had never had a better flautist, certainly while Karajan had been associated with it.

I was still vaguely, and perhaps a little inchoately, obsessed with the rise of J. Galway in the world and with the state of his bank balance. I loved playing with the Berlin Philharmonic, I enjoyed the status, I was happy with the measure of financial security offered me and I was as much under the spell of Karajan as anyone. Yet the grass in the other field still somehow seemed greener. I felt I was not expressing myself fully. I was not my own man. All my stubborn individualism had begun crying out to assert itself, allied to the deep-rooted instincts of a musician who, consciously or unconsciously, feels he is not being heard as he should be.

I had sought to satisfy my longings in this direction by taking on gigs – most of them back in England. Musically, this work proved a source of real pleasure, because as a soloist my flute was rarely heard with the Berlin Phil as anything more than part of a great ensemble. Karajan was preoccupied with mighty things, superb achievements. I on the other hand was like a shepherd on a hillside, wanting merely to play my gentle little instrument. The marvellous, thrilling sounds of Herbie's band increasingly seemed to blot out what I was trying to say.

This was true even in a physical sense. The sounds you hear when you are actually inside a great orchestra are daunting when at full stretch. My second flautist used to stuff wax into his ears to lessen the impact.

The trouble was though, that when I totted up the financial accounts involved in doing gigs and solos outside the orchestra, I realized that my desire for more independence was actually costing me money. Fees for a gig might appear very reasonable. But when the cost of return fares to England was taken into consideration and when I added on top a loss of potential income from the Berlin Phil for the days I was away, it appeared to be costing *me* something like £150 every time I played away. Yet my services were in demand and I also needed the outlet artistically.

One day I was doing a little job in Dublin with the New Irish Chamber Orchestra when Lindsay Armstrong, its manager, who knew all about my problems, remarked, 'Why don't you get yourself an agent, Jimmy?'

'Agents! They're all a bunch of sharks,' I retorted quickly.

'Oh!' said Lindsay and just left it at that.

A day or so later a letter arrived for me from an agent called Michael Emmerson. It was brief and business-like but there was a touch of humour in it that vaguely appealed to me. It read, 'Dear Jimmy, I hear you have a very low opinion of agents as a race and I would like to put this right. Why don't you call and see me sometime?' My immediate reaction was: what a gangster! One day, however, I happened to be sauntering up Regent Street in London when the thought occurred to me: 'Hey, this guy Emmerson works around here. Why don't I go and see him?'

Michael Emmerson and I immediately struck sparks. I was delighted with his honesty and general happiness and outgoing way and from the moment we began talking I knew I could trust him. 'This,' I thought to myself, 'is the guy for me, a guy I can really work with.' There was something in the air between us and since then he and I have never had an argument that lasted more than twenty-four hours. Today, following a stack of successful recordings and more concert appearances than I can count, I am rated a 'star' and introduced on broadcasts and television as 'the world-famous musician' which, for all I know, I may well be. But I did not get there by merely tootling my flute. I had tootled my flute to some purpose with Herbert von Karajan, yet the world, as a whole, knew me not. Under the skilful guidance and direction of Michael Emmerson, however, at long last I began to achieve what I wanted.

None of it, of course, was to happen suddenly or dramatically. Indeed, when Michael began getting me more and more solo engagements and as I began to do less and less with the Berlin Philharmonic, I remarked to him: 'You know, I'm missing out on a bit of money here.' Quick as a flash he came in with the knife. 'Jimmy,' he said, 'if you're ever going to make it, you are going to have to leave the Berlin Philharmonic!'

I looked at him in astonishment. 'Leave the Berlin Phil? That's a big risk – leaving an orchestra like that. I'm now getting around 5,300 Deutschmarks a month basic – and making the same again just fiddling around with solos and gigs. How on earth can I risk all that?'

'Well,' answered Michael steadily, 'if you want me to manage you, if you want to make a career of your own, then you've got to leave the orchestra and take a chance. That's it, cold. There is simply no other way.'

It took two days of solid discussion between us before I made up my mind. Then I returned to Berlin that same weekend and put the problem straight to Annie. Her reaction was predictable. 'Do you think it safe?' she inquired. She pointed out that no one had ever proved himself a successful flute soloist before. The one exception, possibly, was the great Jean-Pierre Rampal who had played everywhere.

'I've *got* to do this, Annie, I've really got to get it together,' I insisted. Very soon after, I began to ease off on my jobs with the Berlin Philharmonic. There was nothing in my contract that obliged me to do recordings or make TV appearances and although I knew that by avoiding certain areas of work I risked annoying Karajan, there was nothing either of us could do about it. I told Herbie that I thought I should leave the orchestra and explained my reasons. He was very nice about it. 'Fine, Jimmy,' he said. 'You leave the orchestra if you feel you have something really worth doing. If you feel you must do something, do it. When I was a youngster there were things I didn't do that I thought I should have done and later I regretted them. And I wouldn't want you to be in the same situation.' I do not honestly know if Karajan really appreciated just how serious I was. He meant his advice sincerely, all right, I don't doubt. But he may have imagined that this was merely an exhibition of temperament and that all he had to do was humour me and that, when I had thought things over, the advantages of staying with him would become apparent.

All I know is that when I officially tendered my resignation in August 1974, to take effect at the end of the season, Herbie almost hit the roof. Nobody resigns from the Berlin Phil. The orchestra is a career in itself and the pension rights alone cannot be dismissed lightly. A little later Lothar Koch came to me and said Herbie had asked him to approach me. 'He told me, "Go and be nice to Jimmy and try to get him to stay in the orchestra," explained Lothar.

'There's no point in being nice to me,' I replied. 'It has nothing to do with people being nice to me or not being nice to me. I simply want to do something else. I want to leave and do something else and that's all there is to it.'

From that point on, my relations with Herbert von Karajan cooled. He thought of the whole orchestra as his family, and anyone daring to consider leaving or standing up to his authority was, to put it at its mildest, not looked upon favourably. Nor was I all that tactful, perhaps, in my own behaviour. During the orchestra's visit to New York that autumn, I asked him if I could have a month's leave to return to Berlin because Annie was expecting a baby. To my surprise, he refused and I considered that pretty rotten of him. Anyway, when I rang Annie and she told me that she was just about to go into hospital, I impetuously decided to take off. I called a taxi and ran downstairs where I saw my friend Nick. I shouted, 'Hey, Nick, can you pay my bill at the hotel? Annie is just off to the hospital and I'm just off to the airport.' I stopped briefly at Carnegie Hall to tell the guys there that my wife was expecting twins and that they would see me back in Berlin.

Relations with Karajan rapidly worsened after that. He is an extremely sensitive and understanding man, yet his behaviour can be diamond-hard whenever he wants it to be. I found myself playing a kind of *coda*; it was as though I were back again in Carnalea Street acting up stroppy with my old dad. Matters came to a head just a few days before the orchestra was about to leave for Salzburg for the Easter Festival.

It is not unknown, of course, for members of an orchestra to treat their conductor in a cavalier way. Karajan is a great gentleman and one of the most charming personalities I have ever known. Yet there are these two sides to his character – one extremely hard, the other extremely charming and soft. He clearly needs a hard side to discipline something like the Berlin Phil because it is a collection of very highly-strung individuals, each with his own good opinion of himself. I recall two guys in the oboe section who are tremendous experts on Bach. They know everything about the great man – the size of shoes he wore, the kind of collar he affected, and they really believe that nobody can play Bach as they can. One day Karajan stopped the orchestra and began explaining how we should play the Bach piece we were then rehearsing. He addressed his remarks principally to these two oboe-players. One of them just stared the Maestro straight in the eye, then made a snoring sound as if he were asleep. Well, Karajan could either shoot him or do what he did – which was to ignore him. I myself have been known to talk back to certain conductors. Once one conductor told me off: 'You know, Galway, that's completely wrong there what you're playing.' I replied, 'Well, if you're going to conduct like that, how do you expect me to play at all!'

Anyhow, in the Philharmonic that day I was busy explaining something to the second flute when Herbie, up on his podium, shouted, 'Hey! First flute!' If our relations had been less cool, I would have undoubtedly behaved with more circumspection. 'Wait a minute!' I yelled back, 'I'm telling the group here something.'

It was like sticking a needle in a tiger. Karajan hit the roof with anger and left the hall without speaking to me. Before I myself could leave, a member of the orchestral committee approached. The committee's function is rather like that of a shop stewards' committee: it is there to negotiate problems between the orchestra on the one hand and the director and management on the other. The committee member passed me the news: Herbie would prefer it if I did not accompany the orchestra to Salzburg for the Easter Festival. The festival is his own, of course, and he had every right to invite who he wished. By refusing to invite me, he was showing how angry he was with me.

Today, of course, we are friends again. When I visited Berlin a year or so later, we patched up our differences completely. Karajan could not have been more charming or friendly and smiled at the recollection of the way we had both behaved, indicating that he realized that he, too, had been temperamental. For the rest of the season, however, I never saw him again nor did I ever play under his baton again.

I left the Berlin Philharmonic in July 1975, six years after

I had first joined it and within a few days had moved family and home to Lucerne where Annie's mother found us a beautiful apartment. Now when I wake in the morning, I can look across the lake and see where Wagner wrote *Tristan and Isolde*; in the little church nearby, his son Siegfried was christened. I cannot think of a better place for a musician to live.

Within a day or so Annie and I moved to the Engelberg where I sat, as already described, and mulled over the problems and difficulties looming ahead of us. However, I did not spend all my time, in thought, or even prayer. Michael Emmerson had arranged that I should perform a solo with the Halle Orchestra, conducted by James Loughran at the Promenade Concerts in the Albert Hall and I also had to prepare two recordings for RCA with whom we had agreed a three-year contract, so I put in an enormous amount of work.

In the event I played the Mozart D Major Concerto at the Albert Hall, music which I had included in my first main recording which later won a *Grand Prix du Disque*. A week after the Promenade Concert I made my first two solo recordings, a sonata disc of Prokofiev and Franck and my 'Showpieces for Flute' with the National Philharmonic Orchestra under Charles Gerhardt.

The Promenade Concert proved a great emotional experience. When I arrived at the Albert Hall, I saw a crowd of Promenaders dressed up in T-shirts which read 'James Galway, the Man with the Golden Flute'. Playing the Proms, of course, is like playing in a vast lunatic asylum with the atmosphere at once unnerving and inspiring. During the first movement, for instance, the kids really became engrossed in the way I handled the difficult technical bits. In the slow movement, their attitude changed profoundly. They stood there with heads bowed, soaking in that gorgeous music. In my own mind I kept thinking: what a marvellous composer this fellow Mozart is. Then my thoughts leaped even further; Mozart is not just a great composer, he has really got the message. He had been truly sent by God. And as I watched those kids, their eyes shining brightly and then saw them standing still and mute, so quiet that you could have heard a pin drop, I knew that my decision to become a soloist had been right.

Nevertheless, concerned for my family's welfare, I was very

much aware that making a career as a solo flautist was a bit like climbing Everest. Michael, however, remained confident. He knew about Rampal and about Severino Gazzelloni, the distinguished Italian flautist, and was convinced that provided I was prepared to work hard and undertake long and arduous tours, I would succeed. Meantime, when I was offered the job of Professor of Flute at the Eastman School of Music in Rochester, New York, I accepted it. I liked teaching young people, but soon realized that I could not pursue my career properly and do justice to the students as well. With more and more concerts and tours on my horizon, it also seemed unfair to Annie to leave her in America with the children, and regretfully I resigned the position after only six months.

Much of the work that Michael had promised me was now beginning to flood in, although at the start I was still prepared to carry out small engagements for minimal fees. All this moving about, however, took my feet off the ground and suddenly I did not know where I was. I found myself in mental disarray and had a series of disturbing and vivid dreams. All my old friends began turning up in these dreams, in the most minute detail, and it seemed that I really wanted to be with these people again and to be associated with old things. For example, I dreamed of Sadler's Wells. It was a tremendous dream. The stage was filled entirely with a huge Buddha. Then I saw myself mingling with my old friends from the orchestra and the dream continued with me walking out of the opera house and boarding a bus with some of them.

I was so disturbed by the recurrence of these dreams that I consulted an analyst who explained that I was disorientated and was missing the reassurance of old friends and familiar places. The Buddha, for instance, represented a desire for peace and repose. Obviously, too, I was still unsure that I could make it as a successful solo artist on the flute. It was not merely my own skill and musicianship that was at stake; the question was would the public, accustomed to solo piano and violin, be easily convinced that the flute was also a solo instrument?

I realized I had turned over many mental and emotional leaves and I did find some degree of peace and repose in my daily readings from the Bible. But I was also being driven by a need to reform myself, following my decision to walk a new road towards God. I found myself spending a lot of time contemplating my situation, both morally and physically. I looked back on my time in Berlin, for example, and probed the reasons for my stroppiness – for the way I had deliberately appeared to set out to shock people with my rock-and-roll clothes and my unorthodox behaviour, and I satisfied myself that much of this had sprung from an inferiority complex.

One day I was talking to an old friend called Shauna Mahlo who for some time worked with the City of Birmingham Symphony Orchestra. She mentioned a teacher and psychoanalyst, Bunty Wills, who she thought might be able to help me. I badly wanted to eliminate some of the rough edges of my relationships with people, to accept people and life more serenely and to learn to be more tolerant. I recognized that I was a bundle of complexes and sensitivities and somehow or other I had to get a more balanced view of myself and of my relationship with others.

I was easily upset, for instance, by little things; even the little mannerisms shown by people with whom I worked. I could not understand why some people could be hostile to me; people to whom, so far as I was aware, I had never done any harm. This lady, who has since worked wonders for me, explained the workings of the mind and when she told me that somebody who irritated me because he constantly talked about money had his own problems, probably reaching back into childhood, this helped me overcome my intolerance and irritability, I was fighting a battle to achieve serenity and placidity, to achieve poise and balance, and to subdue my stormy, impetuous, vaguely undisciplined self. Since then I have become much more charitable towards people. I no longer fly off the handle at the drop of a hat. And my head has been cleared for more productive thoughts.

In just over two years I made six recordings, toured more than twenty countries, appeared on innumerable TV shows and, on 23 November 1976, played at the Royal Concert on St Cecilia's Day before the Queen and Prince Philip in the Royal Albert Hall.

It did all seem a long way from Carnalea Street especially when, in the interval after we had played the Concerto, Mozart, Marisa Robles, the Spanish harpist, and myself were conducted to a small room outside the Royal Box and I was introduced to Her Majesty. For once I was tongue-tied. The Queen did not attempt anything too complex but asked me, as most people do, if it were difficult to play Mozart. I stammered out that it was not difficult to memorize the piece but that nevertheless there were always problems to be faced. In this particular piece I had misjudged my cue and, just before the cadenza in the slow movement, had actually left out two notes. I had turned round, I explained, and was looking at the violins, thinking they were playing so beautifully, that I just forgot I should have started. Prince Philip impressed me as very knowledgeable about music and spoke about how much he loved that particular cadenza. Later, after she had been introduced to the other artists, the Queen returned to me and asked me about Belfast. I did not have much time to go into that situation and I certainly never got around to talking about Alec's bank or Buck Alex or Corky or about guys who kept lions and other interesting memorabilia of the Belfast I knew.

I was keeled over by the reception I received during my tour of South Africa, Australia and Japan. Michael Emmerson's hunch, that in a world dominated by pianos, electric guitars and all sorts of other loud instruments, there had to be space for the pure mellow sound of a flute, proved absolutely right. In Cape Town the applause was so loud and prolonged that I thought: 'This can't have been a flute concerto – I must have played Rachmaninov's Piano Concerto by mistake.' In Japan, where the applause was of the kind normally reserved for bravura performances by pianists, a man came up to me later in the street and said, 'You know, I heard your concert in Cape Town also and I'll never forget it.'

Gradually I was becoming more serene and more happy with myself. I was aware that something called 'success' had begun creeping up on me but I hoped and prayed that it would never in itself mean anything to me. I was not really playing the flute to project Jimmy Galway or even to make money; other than enough, perhaps, to get by, enough to escape worry or to prevent my family suffering. But I had found this relationship with the centre of the universe and I did not intend to let go.

In Lucerne I practised every day, worried a little about my weight, ran quite long distances and played what I call 'Swiss-type tennis' with Annie. My natural bent, perhaps, is to sit around and do nothing except play with the kids, whom I think a scream. They are now into every musical instrument. Patrick bangs drums, blows the flute, pounds the piano with his elbows. Stephen keeps ringing me up from England and saying 'Listen to this, Dad', and then blowing my eardrums off over the telephone with his trumpet. Annie still teaches autistic children but also plays the harpsichord, piano and recorder. In the summer I happily ran my courses for students at Stowe in Buckinghamshire and at Edinburgh. I added to my collection of 18-carat gold flutes made for me by Mr Albert Cooper of Clapham from whom I ordered my first one while I was still playing in Berlin. I enjoy knowing that they are worth £5,000 each but it was not because of their intrinsic value or even through a sense of showmanship that I had bought them. I wanted them because they produce a particular pitch and tone for me.

I had begun to see the whole picture towards the end of 1977 and was becoming more satisfied. All the searching and striving for something that had been beckoning me since I was a kid seemed to be coming to fruition. I was able to smile, laugh, attempt to radiate happiness. I had come to realize how senseless it is to want to possess more material things. Once I used to get wild if the kids got into my gear; now it had ceased to worry me. When I found them using my hi-fi to play their own scratchy records, I accepted it philosophically – although a few years earlier I would have hit the roof.

I had learned to relax, to steer clear of quarrels, to save myself for the work I had to do. I had given up eating meat, convinced that it dulled my senses, dulled my ability to appreciate or to create fantasy. I read eastern philosophies and grew to understand that we are all, in one way or other, seeking the Infinite and that it is wrong to quarrel on the narrow issues. Every day I continued to practise, burying myself in these little segments of notes the way a reader pores over the words of a poem, trying to understand the substance and story behind what was written so that I could make sense of what I was playing.

And then, when I seemed to be finding myself at peace with both God and man and the future bright, something not too far from disaster struck.

CHAPTER FIFTEEN

I had played in the Lucerne Festival for the first time; two concertos, with a Japanese orchestra. The critics were mildly acid with both myself and another rather well-known soloist called Rostropovich which, in my view, said more about the mentality of the critics than the virtuosity or otherwise of Rostropovich and J. Galway. But I shall say nothing further about this, for these days Charity is my middle name.

I was looking forward to another jolly (working) tour in the Mediterranean aboard *The Mermoz* and was busy also with a master class as part of the festival. My views on how to conduct a master class had differed from those of the organizers. They had wanted me to take ten people and put them through a rigorous fortnight. I favoured a different approach which was to take as many people as possible and give them the broad outlines of the idea. The organizers had followed my advice, advertised the class and I was feeling rather pleased with myself, the response had been phenomenal. More than eighty people had applied to take part as players while the number who wished to attend and imbibe the Galway wisdom would have filled the audience seats in a TV studio. You have no idea how good it feels when you realize you have been right about this sort of thing.

Anyhow, because of the large crowd the festival organizers had shifted the venue of the class to a school just outside the town. One day I said to the kids, 'Listen, just a few miles down the road from here, there is someone teaching a class whom I think you should meet. I think we should organize a big outing and go visit him.'

I was referring to Marcel Moyse, whom I regard as the world's finest flautist and to whom my own playing owes much. Although now in his eighties, Moyse leaves Vermont every year to visit friends in France before coming on to Boswil, just outside Lucerne. Here he has been conducting a famous establishment since 1966. I always make a point of dropping in to see him even if only to say 'hello'. One evening, in consequence, we all traipsed down to Boswil. I was driven there by my good friend Phillip Moll, the pianist, who is my only regular recitals partner and with whom I have made several tours and cut many discs.

Afterwards, I sat with Moyse in the Artists' House sipping a glass of wine and talking about possibly visiting him in Vermont. I would have eight days free in the near future and perhaps we could get together and play some Bach sonatas. I have a special regard for the way Moyse plays Bach. Then I took my leave, walked out of the Artist's House and decided to stroll in the mellow warmth of an August evening to a little restaurant five minutes away.

Just outside the house I bumped into a young Japanese flute-player whom I had first met in Tokyo. He was with his girl friend. I asked them if they were going to the restaurant and they said they were, so we decided to go together, the flute-player offering to carry my flutes. En route we were joined by two other people and then by another girl. We were a merry little bunch of minstrels and the thought of tragedy was a long way from our minds.

Suddenly, as we reached a bend in the road near the restaurant, I heard the sound of a motor-bike. There was no pavement and I decided to mount a bank, hoping to keep out of harm's way. The next thing I knew, the Japanese had been struck, then the Dutch girl, and finally the bike went straight over me. I was thrown into the air and ended up in the middle of the road. I did not lose consciousness, but for a second or so was disorientated. Then, as I gathered my wits about me, I realized both my legs were broken and found I had also been knocked completely out of my shoes. I felt no pain and so far as my arms were concerned, they appeared to have been only grazed. Later I was astonished when I was told that my left arm was broken.

We were carted off to the local hospital where we were injected with pain-killing drugs. Through the good offices of my friend Peter Lukas Graf (P. Luke, as we call him, who is also a pupil of Moyse and who played at my wedding) I was moved from the little hospital at Muri to Lucerne where the top Swiss surgeon was available. Muri was too far away for Annie to visit me easily.

Throughout, amazingly, I never worried about my future or about my career. I know now I am lucky to be alive but at the time I thought only of physical problems. I suffer from both astigmatism and myopia and people who have seen me on TV have often asked about my 'dancing eyes' (the cause of this is the harsh TV lighting playing on a congenital ailment.) In the hospital, naturally, they knew nothing about my astigmatism and asked me the same questions over and over again until I began to wonder if they were idiots or if they thought I was the local village nutcase. 'Listen, why do you have to keep asking me the same questions?' I finally demanded in my most stroppy manner.

'After an accident, we have to test to see if there has been any brain damage,' I was told. So on top of broken legs and a broken arm, I now had to worry about my mind. On the other hand, as it seemed to be functioning pretty much as it normally does, I stopped worrying about it and again explained about my astigmatism. In the end, we somehow managed to get this question of whether or not I was off my head erased from the agenda, which was good news.

Not such good news, however, was the little matter of getting me into traction. A hole has to be drilled through your heels and a steel bar inserted and then weights and pulleys hung on this. Two guys were involved in this job and one of them began boring a hole. The other guy watched him for a moment, then remarked, 'You know you're not doing that straight.'

'I know. I can't. I'm far too nervous.' Collapse, more or less, of J. Galway at this point. I felt a lot better, however, when I learned that Professor Vogt, the first Swiss surgeon to sew an arm back on a patient, was in charge of my case and so I knew I was in good hands. It never occurred to me to ask myself whether I would ever play the flute again. Even if the answer had been in the negative, I would not have regarded it as disastrous, for I no longer think in such terms. The flute *is* my life, yet if it were God's will that I should never play it again, then I would hope to resign myself and find another way of earning my living. Nevertheless, I was glad to be told that my arm would knit satisfactorily and that I would be able to play again in eight weeks.

Curious thoughts and reactions do, of course, affect you when you find yourself in sudden trouble. While I was flying through the air, being shot from the bank to the middle of the road, for instance, my life really did flash before my eyes. Nor was I any too charitable towards the motor-cyclist while the ambulance men fussed over us. Certain choice imprecations were visited upon him and I fixed him with the traditional Galway curse so that if he ever gets to heaven, they will hand him a harp with broken strings.

Lying in hospital, however, my experience hardly seemed funny. A few days after the accident, I became extremely depressed. I could no longer even listen to someone singing on the radio. I tuned into an LSO concert in Edinburgh but had to switch off; the contrast between those lucky guys sawing away happily up there in Scotland and me lying in my little Swiss bed, helpless, overwhelmed me. I thought of the last time I had heard *Carmen* which was when I had played with Colin Davis at Sadler's Wells and I contrasted Colin's strength with my own plight. Everything seemed very, very far away from me. I felt isolated, cut-off, vulnerable. Nor was my mental state helped by the thought that for the next ten weeks I would have to lie on my back, unable to move an inch, to left or right. And that I would lie like that, not merely for several hours every day – but for every second of every twenty-four hours of every day during that period.

In the event, the skin peeled off my back so that I constantly seeped blood. The agony was intensified when I found myself sticking to the bandages. Nurses had to scrape gauze away from my raw flesh and I was far from being my usual merry little impish self. Fresh bandages were applied, but every two or three days later the scraping process had to be repeated.

A time arrived, however, when I got used to this and thought: 'Isn't this a good time to go on a diet?' So I restricted my food intake to one bowl of porridge each morning and a vegetarian meal in the middle of the day. Annie visited me daily, bringing the meal with her, and it was at this point I realized what a good friend I had in her; not just a good wife, but a good friend also. This was one of the reasons why I decided to record John Denver's melody, 'Annie' Song' which, to my astonishment, worked itself up to the top of the pop charts. I found the words very nice and thought: 'This is really what I would like to tell my Annie but I can't sing it to her – on the other hand I could play it to her.' I decided it was a way of saying 'thank you' to her.

People who visited me in hospital were astonished to find me apparently looking cheerful. The fact is that I like to keep my troubles to myself for I believe it is every man's duty to put as cheerful a face on himself as possible; we are not here to make others feel miserable.

Eventually, I began to heal and became more like my old self. One day I rang up one of the girls who had been hurt in the same accident and who was in another part of the hospital. 'Guess what?' she announced.

'I can't. What?'

'I got out of bed and walked today.'

'Great!' I said, elated. 'How far did you get?'

'I got as far as the lavatory – all on my own,' she replied triumphantly. Getting out of bed and making the lavatory by yourself was a big thing in hospital. Each day was made up of a succession of such small triumphs – all tiny Mount Everests to those of us involved.

Three months after my admission and when I expected soon to be discharged, Professor Vogt told me, 'I have very bad news for you. I'm afraid I'll have to operate again because your bones are not knitting together properly.'

I had been moving about in a wheelchair for a week or two. In the evenings I was even permitted to leave hospital and go down the road to the local pub for a pint. One evening I went to the pictures. This, therefore, was a terrible blow. The attitude of the hospital staff, however, greatly helped me. Professor Vogt, for instance, told me, 'I could do this operation today (this was on a Thursday) but I'd prefer to do it on Monday and have a good weekend off and be in top trim for it.'

The operation itself lasted almost five hours and when I eventually came round, I thought I had been run over again – this time by a mobile mountain or something equally heavy. Professor Vogt had had to re-set the bones and put in three metal plates, as well as grafting bone from my hip, because some of the breaks had been so badly splintered.

While moving around in the wheelchair, I had already begun practising the flute, but playing a flute is not easy when you are lying on your back. Also a hospital is anything but a restful place. There is always someone coming in to water the plants or change the beds or do something else and I finally hung up a card saying, 'Don't disturb under any circumstances' and settled down to read books on philosophy. And my Bible. One evening, however, I decided to try out two of Bach's unaccompanied sonatas only to have the sister rush in *immediately* and tell me to stop playing because the man next door was trying to sleep – so much for the good intentions lapped-up from my Bible reading.

For a while after the second operation, I allowed myself to toy with the idea that perhaps I might never walk again; that perhaps, the doctors, for all their skill, were wrong. And then, while reading the Bible, I came across a text which talks about 'If you follow in my paths, I will rest your spirit and heal your bones', or words to that effect, and my spirits lifted immediately. Three days before Christmas I was allowed home, still in a wheelchair. Therapy continued for some weeks afterwards but it was March before I was allowed to attempt to walk. Before this, of course, I had recommenced work and was given one of the most joyful and emotional ovations I have ever known when I played the Mozart Flute and Harp Concerto with my friend Marisa Robles in Madrid.

Still in my wheelchair, I did a programme for BBC TV in the *World of Music* series which I found very exhausting, but which was very well received – and even repeated some months later. All the time, though, I kept cheering myself up by reminding myself that if I had been involved in a similar accident a half-century previously, I would have been confined to a wheelchair for the rest of my life. The miracle of modern surgery had saved me from that fate.

Out of the travail, I believe, came benefits. My awareness of spiritual values was enhanced. For a while, too, I had managed to get my head out of the whole publicity machine, and was able to appreciate what it could do to me if I was not careful.

When I realized that I was in hospital for an extended stay, I had installed a hi-fi set and had settled down to listen to all the records I normally never get a chance to hear; the list, I should mention, included a number of pop records. I sometimes think it funny that as a kid I would never go to dances – although you couldn't keep brother George away from them – because I had this snobbish attitude towards popular music and thought that I should never listen to dance tunes because they were rubbish.

Not that I do not still remain closely wedded to classical music, of course. In hospital I also listened to such people as Artur Rubinstein and Maria Callas for hours on end. One day, Michael Emmerson arrived in Lucerne with a pile of John Denver cassettes which he thought I might enjoy. While listening to them I suddenly realized that these were very good songs – that they made you feel great. Then I heard John Denver announce 'Annie's Song' – the record was taped from a live performance at the London Palladium – and heard him declare, 'I'd like to dedicate this song to my wife because she's beautiful. It's called "Annie's Song" because that is the name of my wife.' When I heard it, I decided I would like to play it for my Annie – and did. And so there we were. On top of everything else, J. Galway was being hailed as a pop star.

And Annie? She was very pleased, of course, when 'her song' climbed to the top of the charts. Yet her reaction was more one of mild embarrassment than anything else, although I do know she appreciated the gesture.

So far as I was concerned, the record had achieved all of its objectives. I had expressed my love for my wife in the most fluent way available to me; by speaking to her with my music.

For myself, the accident heightened and reinforced the attitudes that had finally crystallized for me upon the Engelberg. I decided that henceforward I would play every concert, cut every record, give every TV performance, as though it were my last. I have come to understand that it is never possible to guess what might happen next; that the roof might fall in any time and that the important thing is to make sure that every time I play the flute my performance will be as near perfection and full of true music as God intended and that I shall not be remembered for a shoddy performance. My ambitions, therefore, are limited. They are merely that I should leave good memories behind me; that people should feel when they recall my name, that in some odd inexplicable way, they have at sometime heard the voice of the Infinite through me.